No ordi
season

Rob Fielding

ISBN: 978-1-291-42689-2

About the author

Rob Fielding's first Port Vale game was a home match against Lincoln City back in 1980. John McGrath's side managed to lose 1-0, a result that, he claims, prepared him for life as a Vale fan.

In the mid-1990's, he was a recent graduate, without much money, based in Bristol. He created a Port Vale website called "There's only one Vale fan in Bristol?" as a way of getting lift shares from fellow supporters based in the West Country. Over the years, that site evolved into onevalefan.co.uk (or OVF for short) a popular, award-winning Port Vale fan site.

As OVF editor, he has been in an ideal position to chronicle the events of the extraordinary 2012-2013 season.

Thanks

I would like to thank my wife, Jo, for her help, assistance and motivational advice ("just get on with it").

I would also like to thank: everyone who proofread the manuscript and helped correct my errors; Paine Proffitt for kindly allowing his amazing Port Vale artwork to adorn the front of the book; the fans who allowed their photographs to be used throughout the book and everyone else who has contributed to this book. Any remaining errors are the author's own.

Photos on the back cover of this book by kind permission of: Rob Machin, Barry Bevington, Alex Woolgar and Pete Tindall.

This book is dedicated to my dad – the "owd" Vale fan.

Money from the sale of each book will be donated to Stoke-on-Trent charities and good causes.

Contents

Prologue: a false dawn **9**

August: 'rock bottom' **15**

September: feed the Pope and... **33**

October: new hope **53**

November: Roy, Rovers and revival **77**

December: ending the year on a high **103**

January: new year, new additions **117**

February: nerves start to jangle **137**

March: a serious 'blip' **153**

April: finishing the job **179**

Appendix

OVF player of the season **209**

National awards **210**

Player of the year awards **211**

Pope's records **212**

Trivia **213**

Player stats **214**

Player profiles **215**

"Failure or success seems to have been allotted to men from the stars. But they retain the power of wriggling, of fighting with their star or against it and in the whole universe the only really interesting movement is that wriggle."

- E.M Forster

"Football. Bloody hell!"

- Sir Alex Ferguson

Prologue: a false dawn

"In some ways this is a very sad matter. The sale of a football club is never easy. Hopefully when it rises it will flourish."

- High Court Judge Sir Jonathan Baker QC at the club's administration application, 14th April, 2012

"It will be the perfect administration if true."

– BBC *Sport*'s Matt Slater comments on remarks by administrator Gerald Krasner that a deal could be struck by the end of April

"We're hoping that we can bring a bit of sunshine."

– Keith Ryder speaking on 6 Towns radio, 18th April

"I hope we can complete all of the necessary paperwork at the earliest opportunity to complete the deal as swiftly as possible."

- Keith Ryder, 27th April

Keith Ryder addresses the fans after a Supporters Club meeting
[Photo: AS Photos]

"It should now be done and dusted, I don't see any obstacles."

- Administrator Bob Young on the Keith Ryder takeover, 14th July

If you were a Vale supporter on the 14th July 2012, you'd probably be feeling quite happy. The Valiants appeared to be finally poised to exit the dark days of board mismanagement, anti-board protests and supporter unrest and enter an exciting, prosperous era under new owner Keith Ryder. Surely, no Vale fan would have guessed just how differently events turned out...

Firstly, let's take a brief step back in time to explain the events that lead to that Bob Young announcement on the 14th July.

Port Vale Football club had entered administration for the second time in their history on the 14th April 2012. There had been months of protests against what was widely regarded to be a self-serving and incompetent board and it was clear that something had to give. Finally, the board, prompted by a winding-up petition by HM Revenue & Customs, applied for administration.

The club was duly placed in the hands of administrators Begbies Traynor and within seven days of the hearing, chief administrator Bob Young told the press that there were already six parties interested in the club.

Despite the loss of three key players (striker Marc Richards, winger Sean Rigg and midfielder Anthony Griffith) the future still looked bright. The administration process looked straightforward and the fans expected a new owner to be in place soon.

On the 4th April 2012, Lancashire businessman Keith Ryder was named as the club's preferred bidder. Little was known about Ryder, but talks with the Supporters Club were hailed as "constructive and amicable." From the outside, the future looked bright for the Valiants. Surely the deal would be completed quickly and new signings could then be brought in to replace those who had already left?

However, the Ryder takeover dragged on as the Football League refused to sanction the deal without more information from the potential new owner. Ryder said he'd provide more details and insisted that the deal would be completed by the end of June.

That deadline passed, but on the 14th July, Bob Young issued the optimistic statement that the takeover should be "done and dusted." Fans could be forgiven for breathing a sigh of relief.

But of course, Ryder failed to make that 14th July deadline. And the 20th July deadline. And the 24th July deadline.

Finally, it dawned on the fans that the takeover was not going to happen and the club would have to start the season in administration. Ryder had promised much but had delivered nothing, apart from another false dawn for frustrated Port Vale supporters.

August: 'rock bottom'

"The coronation of Keith Ryder as the club's new owner once looked a formality but at time of writing it still hasn't happened. Events have reached farcical proportions as Ryder continues to promise to conclude the deal in 24 hours and Vale fans worry that the club may have to start the season in administration and running out of money."

– Rob Fielding's season preview for the *Guardian*

"A summer which has seen faffing about taken to a new level… the lengthy delays do not auger well for our future."

– Fanzine *Derek I'm Gutted's* take on the administration

"The football club has hit rock-bottom."

– Manager Micky Adams, 13th August

After the collapse of the Keith Ryder takeover, it wasn't surprising that the club began preparations for the new season in complete disarray as one crisis after another occurred.

On the 2nd August, the Supporters Club revealed that Ryder had stopped returning their calls as the administrators started to look at alternative options. Ryder's exclusivity as the "preferred bidder" had expired at the end of July and the club was now free to consider other bids from interested parties.

On the same day, the club announced that friendlies may have to take place behind closed doors as safety work had not taken place (a statement subsequently condemned as "pathetic" by the Supporters Club).

To complete a thoroughly miserable day, the city council, who were underwriting the club's administration declared themselves "disappointed" with the takeover delays. As the Port Vale fanzine *Derek I'm Gutted* put it – "It's now clear we're in the s**t."

Bob Young, one of the administrators charged with running
the club pictured at a Supporters meeting [Photo: AS Photos]

At least the problems with Vale Park were quickly resolved after the Supporters Club appealed for volunteers to come forward and help the club get the ground prepared for the new season. As a result, on the 3rd August, Bob Young told the *Sentinel* that Vale had assured the Football League that the ground would be ready in time for the new season.

But although the stadium was now ready, would any of the remaining players make an appearance on it?

Vale had strengthened their squad in the summer in the expectation that the Ryder deal would be completed. But the protracted mess of the takeover had left most of Vale's playing staff on revised month-to-month deals rather than the one or two year deals that they had originally signed.

On the 6th August, manager Micky Adams told the *Sentinel* that the Valiants would be able to field a team against Burnley because the revised contracts had been approved by the Football League. But the manager's optimism was to be sorely tested as the club plunged into another fresh crisis.

In a topsy-turvy twenty four hours, initially there was good news from the club. On the 8th August Bob Young announced that he had managed to amend players' contracts from month-to-month deals to longer deals, stretching initially to the end of the season with the originally agreed contract lengths being honoured when new owners eventually take over.

This was widely welcomed as the shorter monthly agreements could have allowed players to leave with the minimum of notice. Young's move looked to have secured the players for this season, at least.

But Young had spoken prematurely. New deals may have been on the table, but that didn't mean that they would be signed and the following day, events took a worrying turn for the worse.

The players were, by now, understandably concerned about their futures, given the instability of the club, and announced that they would not sign the new deals until they had talks with the Professional Footballers Association (the PFA). There was now the possibility of a mass exodus of players on the very eve of the season.

Vale had just four days to resolve the mess as the club would have to register its squad on the 13th August in time for the first game of the season.

To huge relief, following talks led by the club's PFA rep Gareth Owen, seventeen of the eighteen players showed great loyalty to the Valiants and agreed to stay. David Artell, alone, decided to leave for the security of a contract with Northampton.

The announcement that contracts had been agreed was made during the final friendly game against Tranmere Rovers and the remaining members of the Vale squad received a deserved standing ovation from the Vale supporters present.

But yet again, with one crisis averted, another one came to the fore. While the club was awaiting the expected completion of the Ryder deal, no kit deal had been agreed for the new season.

The Vale team observe a minute's silence (above) and warm-up (below) ahead of a friendly with Galway – most players remained loyal to the club throughout administration [Photos: K.Walshaw]

Just days ahead of the opening clash with Burnley it was revealed that a "temporary" kit deal had been arranged, but the suppliers were unable to supply the kit in Vale's traditional black and white colours. To general amusement and some criticism, the club announced that the team would play their first home match of the season in a bright pink strip! Thankfully, a more traditional black and white outfit would be available a few weeks later.

So, at least the club had (thanks to the efforts of those volunteers) a ground fit for purpose, the majority of the players were willing to play for Port Vale and there was a temporary (albeit pink) kit to play in.

Now, there was just the small matter of the season proper with crisis-hit Vale 18th favourites to win promotion.

Match One
Opposition: At home to Burnley
Competition: Capital One Cup, round 1
Date: August 14, 2012
Scoreline: Port Vale 1-3 Burnley
Vale goal: Shuker (9 mins)
Attendance: 4,055

Pre-match quote: "I hope the football club has hit rock-bottom and we can start to climb again, but I can't guarantee that." (Micky Adams)

Port Vale line-up: Neal, Yates, McCombe, Davis (McDonald), Loft, Myrie-Williams, Shuker (Burge), Morsy, Vincent (Williamson), Dodds, Pope

Match report snippet: "With all Port Vale's protracted off-field woes, it was a relief to concentrate on matters on the pitch and a respectable crowd of just over 4,000 were there to watch proceedings." (OVF)

OVF man of the match: Doug Loft

Post-match quote: "It was always going to be tough against Burnley. They are a good side and have spent a lot of money. We won't be playing against that calibre of player against Barnet on Saturday, but we still have to make sure our defending is better and that we do the basics." (Micky Adams)

Chris Shuker in action during a friendly against Alsager. Shuker scored the club's first goal of the season [Photo: AS Photos]

"All four [bidders] have good intentions, as far as I can tell, and they are all using well-known firms of solicitors. That's a good sign and usually indicative that someone is serious about making a bid. I had never heard of Keith's solicitors before we started dealing with them."

- Bob Young's rather unconventional way of assessing "serious" bidders, 16th August

There was a general feeling of relief after the Burnley game. Even though the Vale had lost and were out of the cup, at least the club had managed to successfully fulfil its first fixture of the season.

There was a glimmer of hope off the pitch too. Bob Young told the *Sentinel* that there were now four parties interested in the club.

Now it was time for the Vale's first league games of the season: a home match against Barnet and two days later, a trip to Accrington.

Match Two
Opposition: At home to Barnet
Competition: League Two
Date: August 18, 2012
Scoreline: Port Vale 3-0 Barnet
Vale goals: Dodds (8), Myrie-Williams (20 pen), Pope (75)
Attendance: 4,608

Pre-match quote: "If we give them time and space, they'll enjoy coming here again, and we can't afford that." (Micky Adams)

Port Vale line-up: Neal, Duffy (Yates), McCombe, McDonald, Loft, Myrie-Williams, Shuker (Burge), Morsy, Vincent (Williamson), Dodds, Pope

Match report snippet: "Port Vale sealed a comfortable opening-day victory over disappointing Barnet. Louis Dodds volleyed Vale ahead in the eighth minute before former Stevenage winger Jennison Myrie-Williams stroked home a 20th minute penalty, awarded when Tom Pope was fouled by Jon Nurse." (BBC)

OVF man of the match: Louis Dodds

Post-match quote: "We're pleased with the three points, because that's all it is. I am delighted with some of the play today and disappointed with some also, but all in all I've got to be happy." (Micky Adams)

Match Three
Opposition: Away at Accrington
Competition: League Two
Date: August 21, 2012
Scoreline: Accrington 2-0 Port Vale
Vale goals: none
Attendance: 1,946 (581 away)

Pre-match quote: "It was obviously a traumatic pre-season and I was wondering whether the spirit would be right. But we put that to bed on Saturday. We were excellent in that respect. The off-field problems are something of a recurring nightmare, but it's no excuse for what happens on the field." (Micky Adams)

Port Vale line-up: Neal, Duffy (Yates), McCombe, McDonald, Loft, Myrie-Williams, Shuker (Burge), Morsy, Vincent (Williamson), Dodds, Pope

Match report snippet: "2-0 flattered Stanley but Vale didn't take two late chances and paid the price." (Lancashire Telegraph)

OVF man of the match: Doug Loft

Post-match quote: "It just wasn't our night in the end, I suppose. We outplayed Accrington for large spells of the game, but they rode their luck and it's their night." (Micky Adams)

"Do I think that Micky Adams can bring us success in the coming season? Yes, I believe he can. He seems to have the backing of a good group of players."

- Would these be prophetic words? OVF blogger Malcolm Hirst, 23rd August

In the week following the Accrington defeat there were more encouraging noises from the club's administrators. Bob Young told the *Sentinel* that they would be expecting at least "one concrete bid" from the four parties interested in the club.

But as the weekend approached, fans' thoughts turned to events on the pitch and a journey to Morecambe.

Match Four
Opposition: Away at Morecambe
Competition: League Two
Date: August 25, 2012
Scoreline: Morecambe 1-3 Port Vale
Vale goals: Morsy (1), McCombe (89), Pope (90)
Attendance: 2,146 (641 away)

Pre-match quote: "I don't think I've ever had an easy game against Morecambe while Jim Bentley has been in charge. And he's certainly not one of those managers you want to pick a fight with, particularly if you're only 5ft 8in, like me." (Micky Adams)

Port Vale line-up: Neal, Duffy, McCombe, McDonald, Loft, Myrie-Williams (Taylor), Shuker (Murphy), Morsy, Vincent, Dodds (Williamson), Pope

Match report snippet: "The Shrimps were undone by a late Port Vale smash and grab raid." (Lancaster Guardian)

OVF man of the match: Sam Morsy

Post-match quote: "I thought we were excellent and fully deserved the win." (Micky Adams)

Despite the excellent performance against Morecambe, Micky Adams wasn't entirely happy with his squad. Defender Clayton McDonald had come into the side after Joe Davis had a rocky game against Burnley and Adams somewhat surprisingly pulled no punches over McDonald's performances.

"In many respects Clayton has been lucky to get his chance," Adams told the *official Port Vale website*. "He has come in and done reasonably well, but I feel there are certain aspects of his game he can improve on. I certainly want to see his fitness levels improve further and I think he can do something with his weight as well."

It seemed an odd remark to make as McDonald's performances had gone down well with the fans. Perhaps it was just the manager's way of motivating one of the remaining members of his small squad?

Meanwhile, rumours were circulating that Mike Newton, who had expressed an interest in taking over the Valiants in 2010, was preparing a bid for the club. Newton announced his departure from the Oldham Athletic board on August 28th but the US-based businessman denied the move had anything to do with a bid for the Vale.

"Contrary to what some may think, I am not looking to buy Port Vale FC, though I want to remain in football in some capacity," Newton told the *Oldham Chronicle* newspaper.

So, while it had been a good start on the pitch, off it things were far less certain. With one potential bidder ruled out, Vale fans would have to wait to find out who, if anyone, wanted to own their club.

The League Two table: end of August

	Club	GD	Points
1	Oxford Utd	+5	9
2	Gillingham	+4	9
3	Cheltenham	+3	7
4	Bradford	+3	6
5	**PORT VALE**	**+3**	**6**

September: feed the Pope and...

"Popey looks sharper and fitter than he's ever been as a Vale player and if he stays injury and trouble free I honestly think we could have a 25 goal plus striker on our hands."

- Columnist Martin Tideswell, 14th September

"Let's face it, he likes a pint. But he's had a fantastic pre-season and I think I've got him as fit as I possibly can."

– Micky Adams on Tom Pope, 10th September

"In the 38 years since I first became an insolvency practitioner I have never been in such a scenario before where you get so far down the line and a party disappears."

- Bob Young on the Keith Ryder situation, 1st September

Following the trauma of the previous month, Vale started September in much better heart. Fans had become reconciled to the administrators running the club for a while longer, while a decent start to the season had eased fears of a potential relegation to the non-league circuit. Now, it was down to the team to build on their decent opening to the season.

The club's administrators were still confident of buyers for the club with three parties "taking it very seriously" according to Bob Young. But Young also added a word of caution adding that "there is no urgency with the time scale now the season has started. It is more important we get it right."

After suffering the Keith Ryder fiasco, Vale fans couldn't agree more.

Match Five
Opposition: At home to Torquay United
Competition: League Two
Date: September 1, 2012
Scoreline: Port Vale 1-1 Torquay
Vale goals: Saah (69, own-goal)
Attendance: 4,721

Pre-match quote: "We won't be spending £10m on a player, so if you're a Torquay supporter, I advise you to have a nice relaxing meal tonight, rather than sitting in front of the telly." (with the match coming after the hyperbole of transfer deadline day, Torquay boss Martin Ling is refreshingly realistic)

Port Vale line-up: Neal, Duffy, McCombe, McDonald, Loft, Myrie-Williams, Morsy, Shuker (Burge), Dodds (Williamson), Vincent (Taylor), Pope

Match report snippet: "Micky Adams must hope it was just one of those days as his side battered Torquay... only to emerge with a 1-1 draw thanks to a bizarre Brian Saah own goal." (Sentinel)

OVF man of the match: Sam Morsy

Post-match quote: "But for one bit of sloppy defending we did everything but win the game." (Micky Adams)

Match Six
Opposition: At home to Tranmere Rovers
Competition: Johnstone's Paints Trophy
Date: September 4, 2012
Scoreline: Port Vale 2-0 Tranmere Rovers
Vale goals: Myrie-Williams (57, 75 pen)
Attendance: 2,702

Pre-match quote: "We would love a run in this cup again. We will put out a team as strong as possible for a tough match." (Vale assistant manager Mark Grew)

Port Vale line-up: Neal, Duffy (Yates), McCombe, McDonald, Loft, Myrie-Williams, Shuker, Morsy (Burge), Vincent, Dodds (Williamson), Pope

Match report snippet: "Jennison Myrie-Williams blasted Vale into the second round of the Johnstone's Paint Trophy with two goals – a thumping free kick and a penalty." (Liverpool Echo)

OVF man of the match: Jennison Myrie-Williams

Post-match quote: "At times we looked very, very good..." (Micky Adams)

"Mr Young and Mr Currie no longer believe that Mr Ryder is in a position to complete the deal and have no option but to consider the deal dead."

- A joint statement by the administrators and Supporters Club 7th September

The win over Tranmere stretched Vale's unbeaten run to three games, but off the pitch progress was still slow.

One bright spot was the publication of new fortnightly joint statements from the administrators and the Supporters Club – a sensible initiative giving fans regular and joined-up information about what was going on.

The first statement announced that after numerous attempts to contact Keith Ryder, the club's administrators had now declared the deal "dead." As fanzine *Derek I'm Gutted* put it, this was "probably one of the more unnecessary press releases."

The administrators were happier with events on the pitch. Begsbie-Traynor had informed the Supporters Club that the club needed attendances of 5,000 to break-even and although the crowds had been slightly below that figure, things still looked promising.

And following the next home game against Rotherham, Vale's fortunes on the pitch would get even better...

Match Seven
Opposition: At home to Rotherham United
Competition: League Two
Date: September 8, 2012
Scoreline: Port Vale 6-2 Rotherham
Vale goals: Dodds (5), Pope (16, 21, 68, 78), Vincent (28)
Attendance: 5,544

Pre-match quote: "Off the pitch it's carnage at Port Vale and I feel sorry for Micky Adams. They've got a good team though and I think Ashley Vincent and Tom Pope are excellent strikers and they're a handful for any defence." (prophetic words from Rotherham boss Steve Evans)

Port Vale line-up: Neal, Duffy, McCombe, McDonald (Owen), Loft, Myrie-Williams (Taylor), Shuker, Morsy, Vincent (Williamson), Dodds, Pope

Match report snippet: "This was a big shock to the system. Of course, rubbing it all in were the four goals from Tom Pope - the same number he managed in more than 50 league games for Rotherham!" (Sheffield Star)

OVF man of the match: Tom Pope

Post-match quote: "The forward play was the best I've seen in a long time... and the first forty five minutes was probably the best football Vale fans have seen in a while." (Micky Adams)

"He's always had a questionable lifestyle. Let's face it, he likes a pint. But he's had a fantastic pre-season and I think I've got him as fit as I possibly can, and he's reaping the rewards of that."

- Micky Adams on striker Tom Pope, 10th September

Following his four goal haul against Rotherham, media interest in Tom Pope intensified and in an interview with the *Sentinel*, Pope explained how a new attitude had helped to sharpen him up for the new season.

"I hadn't had a full pre-season for three years and I've never had one like that I've just been through," Pope told the newspaper. "I knew it was going to be tough so I did a lot of work on my own while others went on their holidays. I probably surprised a few people."

Meanwhile, assistant manager Mark Grew paid credit to the Vale fans as he commented: "The supporters have been fantastic."

Tom Pope pictured in pre-season action against Nantwich Town
[Photo: onevalefan.co.uk]

There was further good news for the club with the announcement that the win over Rotherham had won the League Managers' Association's performance of the week award.

Next up for the Valiants were two tricky away trips – firstly to Plymouth then a trip to big-spending Fleetwood. If Vale could get good results from those two fixtures then things really were starting to look up.

Match Eight
Opposition: Away at Plymouth Argyle
Competition: League Two
Date: September 15, 2012
Scoreline: Plymouth 1-3 Port Vale
Vale goals: Myrie-Williams (66 pen), Vincent (74), Williamson (78)
Attendance: 6,080 (203 away)

Pre-match quote: "I'm not surprised at all where Port Vale are in the table. I thought they were a very good side last season and that hasn't changed this year. They have got some good players and the way Micky Adams has got them set up is working really well for them." (Plymouth boss Carl Fletcher compliments the Valiants)

Port Vale line-up: Neal, Duffy, McCombe, McDonald, Loft, Myrie-Williams, Morsy, Shuker (Burge), Vincent (Taylor), Pope, Dodds (Williamson)

Match report snippet: "Port Vale were much improved in the second period and netted three times in only 12 minutes to take complete control of the game." (Plymouth Herald)

OVF man of the match: Jennison Myrie-Williams

Post-match quote: "Ashley and Jennison were outstanding in the second half." (Micky Adams)

Match Nine
Opposition: Away at Fleetwood
Competition: League Two
Date: September 18, 2012
Scoreline: Fleetwood 2-5 Port Vale
Vale goals: Pope (29,60), Dodds (67,78), Vincent (34)
Attendance: 3,392 (1,139 away)

Pre-match quote: "I've not changed the side for seven games, but that doesn't mean to say the other players are not in my thoughts." (Micky Adams)

Port Vale line-up: Neal, Duffy, McCombe, McDonald, Loft, Myrie-Williams (Williamson), Morsy (Burge), Shuker, Vincent (Taylor), Pope, Dodds

Match report snippet: "Strikers Louis Dodds and Tom Pope both scored twice as Micky Adam's free-scoring Vale secured an astonishing 5-2 away win over Fleetwood Town." (OVF)

OVF man of the match: Jennison Myrie-Williams

Post-match quote: "It was everything we wanted it to be. I didn't expect it and we certainly had to work hard for it. Every time we went forward, we looked like we would cause Fleetwood problems and it was definitely our attacking play, rather than our defending, which got us through." (Micky Adams)

By now, Vale's attacking play, involving wingers Myrie-Williams and Vincent, was attracting attention and the system was working as striker Tom Pope told the *Sentinel*.

"The front four look like they have played together for years," he said. "Me and Doddsy have been scoring, while Ash and Jennison are ripping teams apart."

Despite the team gelling on the pitch, things were still up in the air off it. A further joint-statement from the administrators and Supporters Club on the 20th September claimed that seven parties were interested in the club and everyone was "working hard" to secure an "acceptable bid" In a magnanimous gesture, the club's administrators revealed that they had exceeded their funding cap but due to the circumstances they would not be claiming any further money for the additional time running the club.

Meanwhile, the administrators confirmed that they had been working with police who had been investigating the activities of former board members.

Administrator Steve Currie commented: "We continue to look at a number of areas where we may be able to recover funds – including the issuing of 'nil-paid' shares."

Next up on the pitch was the visit of table-topping Gillingham with Vale fans keen to see how their side fared against Martin Allen's League Two pacesetters.

Match Ten
Opposition: Home to Gillingham
Competition: League Two
Date: September 22, 2012
Scoreline: Port Vale 0-2 Gillingham
Vale goals: none
Attendance: 6,978

Pre-match quote: "The manager will force them forward and they look a decent side who are a real threat to us. But if we beat them we go top, so it's all to play for." (Micky Adams)

Port Vale line-up: Neal, Duffy, McCombe, McDonald, Loft, Myrie-Williams, Morsy (Taylor), Shuker (Burge), Vincent, Dodds (Williamson) , Pope

Match report snippet: "Micky Adams' side lost their first home league game of the season after they were defeated 2-0 by table-topping Gillingham in front of a near 7,000 crowd." (OVF)

OVF man of the match: Chris Neal

Post-match quote: "I'll go home disappointed by some of my own thinking for the Gillingham game, and I'm big enough to say that." (Micky Adams)

The home defeat rocked Vale somewhat and manager Micky Adams confirmed that he may look to change his starting eleven after playing the same side for nine consecutive matches.

There was mixed news for the Vale midfield: Ryan Burge, who had been transfer-listed over the summer, said he was willing to commit his future to the club after recovering from an "injury nightmare" but somewhat ironically, summer signing Darren Murphy, a rival for Burge in the starting line-up, was injured in a reserve clash.

There was further bad news with Micky Adams hinting that luckless winger Lewis Haldane may not feature for the club again. Haldane, who had suffered a number of injuries since joining Vale, was attempting to recover from a horrendous double leg fracture sustained the previous season but was clearly struggling to make a complete recovery.

On the 26th September, administrator Bob Young told the Sentinel newspaper that the club was in "advanced talks" with "three definite front-runners" bidding to takeover the club. Young also added that he was confident of "a deal progressing within a month."

As the month drew to a close, it was time for Vale to visit Bradford City for their League Two clash. Would they be able to bounce back from their Gills defeat and continue their fine away form?

Match Eleven
Opposition: Away to Bradford
Competition: League Two
Date: September 29, 2012
Scoreline: Bradford 0-1 Port Vale
Vale goals: Pope (37)
Attendance: 11,030 (661 away)

Pre-match quote: "We're going to have to push ourselves mentally and physically. Port Vale work very hard for each other and are very committed, like we are." (Bradford manager Phil Parkinson)

Port Vale line-up: Neal, Duffy (Yates), McDonald, McCombe, Taylor, Myrie-Williams, Loft, Burge, Vincent (Morsy), Pope, Dodds

Match report snippet: "Port Vale still prove to be an annoying thorn in the side. It is now six years since they were last beaten in open play at Valley Parade." (Bradford Telegraph and Argus)

OVF man of the match: Chris Neal

Post-match quote: "To come away with a 1-0 win feels like I've been to the sweet shop and nicked a few sweets, to be honest." (Micky Adams)

As September ended, Vale were still no nearer discovering who would want to own the club. But on the pitch, the excellent start to the season had resulted in the Valiants being placed in second position.

Despite the good start on the pitch, fans were still anxious: would Micky Adams be able to keep his key players with the club so desperately short of money? What would happen if injuries or suspensions hit Vale's miniscule squad? Could Tom Pope continue his scoring form? And would the club survive long enough for new owners to be found?

League Two table: end of September

	Club	GD	Points
1	Gillingham	+12	22
2	**Port Vale**	**+11**	**19**
3	Fleetwood	+6	17
4	Accrington	+4	17
5	Exeter	+5	16

October: new hope

"I never quite got to the stage of hanging out the bunting and worshipping at the feet of Keith Ryder and it's for similar reasons, that I feel that 'cautious optimism' should again be the byword following the announcement that Paul Wildes is the club's preferred bidder."

– Rob Fielding's blog on OVF, 17th October

"Well, he turned up – which is a start."

– Columnist Martin Tideswell on Paul Wildes, 17th October

It was perhaps a portent of things to come that October started on a positive note with a Help For Heroes night during the home fixture against Dagenham.

What was the Help for Heroes night?

The onevalefan.co.uk (OVF) website had received a message that two Vale fans served in the RAF and were returning from service in Afghanistan. The pair, Steve Buffey and Pete Blakeman would be going to the Dagenham game, which would be their first game of the season.

OVF editor Rob Fielding wanted to do something to mark the occasion and approached the club for their help in organizing a night to remember.

It was a measure of the new unity between the club and fans that Port Vale FC pulled out all the stops to make the Dagenham game the 'Help for Heroes' night, welcoming Buffey and Blakeman as guests of honour and helping to raise over £850 for the Help for Heroes charity.

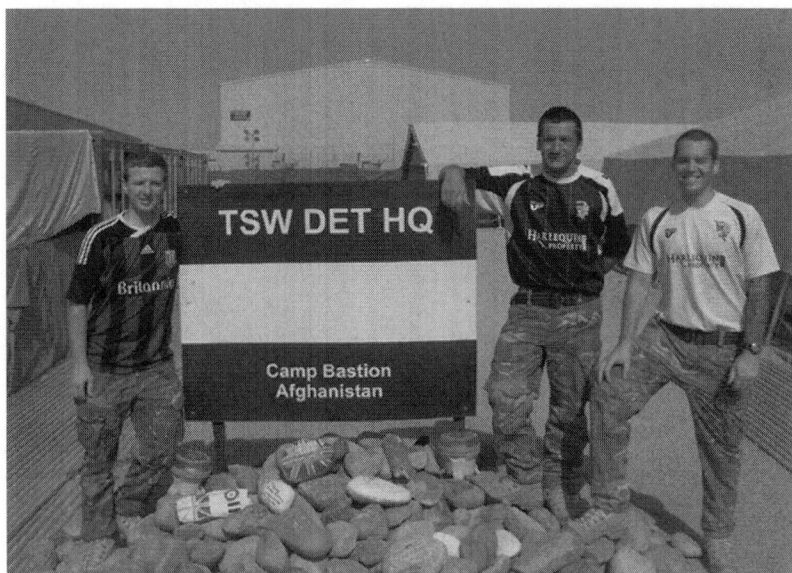

This photo, showing Steve Buffy (centre) and Pete Blakeman (right) prompted OVF to organize the Help For Heroes night

Pete Blakeman and Steve Buffey at the Dagenham game
[Photos: Steve Buffey and Gerard Austin]

Match Twelve
Opposition: Home to Dagenham
Competition: League Two
Date: October 2, 2012
Scoreline: Port Vale 1-1 Dagenham
Vale goals: Myrie-Williams (75)
Attendance: 4,355

Pre-match quote: "It doesn't matter if you are playing Dagenham and Redbridge or Manchester United, you have to go out and set your stall and do everything right." (Clayton McDonald)

Port Vale line-up: Neal, Duffy (Yates), McCombe, McDonald, Loft, Myrie-Williams, Morsy, Burge (Shuker), Vincent, Dodds (Williamson), Pope

Match report snippet: "Dagenham's Luke Howell scored after 72 minutes when his shot squirmed through the legs of home goalkeeper Chris Neal only for Jennison Myrie-Williams to equalise for the Valiants two minutes later." (London 24)

OVF man of the match: John McCombe

Post-match quote: "Chris [Neal] has been magnificent all season. It's unfortunate that when keepers make mistakes it usually costs goals, but I'm sure he'll learn from it and I'm sure he'll bounce back." (Micky Adams)

On the 4th October there was a further joint-statement from the administrators and Supporters Club. The statement began by announcing that there were now three "front runners" bidding to take over the club but there was also the welcome news that the long-awaited Roy Sproson statue would be unveiled on the 17th November.

The Sproson statue – a tribute to Vale legend

The sixteen-foot statue pays tribute to Vale legend Roy Sproson and his family. One-club man Roy made 837 starts (plus 5 sub appearances) for the club and also managed the side. Perhaps uniquely in the game of football, Roy's brother Jess also made 38 appearances for the Vale while Roy's nephew, Phil, made 495 starts (plus 5 sub appearances).

To pay tribute to the family, the Sproson Fund was created to raise funds for a permanent memorial, a statue, in honour of Roy and his family. With help from the Supporters Club, the £96,000 needed to fund the statue was raised thanks to over eleven years of painstaking fund-raising activity.

The erection of the statue was due to take place in December 2011, but the ceremony was cancelled when the then-board refused to offer hospitality to the Sproson family. The Supporters Club cancelled the unveiling in protest and the formal unveiling of the statue was delayed until after the board had departed Vale Park.

Match Thirteen
Opposition: Away to Exeter
Competition: League Two
Date: October 6, 2012
Scoreline: Exeter 0-2 Port Vale
Vale goals: Pope (40, 62)
Attendance: 3,938 (262 away)

Pre-match quote: "If we can keep him [Cureton] quiet, we're halfway to getting a result." (Micky Adams)

Port Vale line-up: Neal, Duffy, McDonald, McCombe, Taylor, Myrie-Williams (Lloyd), Loft (Burge), Morsy, Vincent (Shuker), Dodds, Pope

Match report snippet: "Vale displayed the kind of pace and trickery on the flanks that has unlocked the majority of defences they have come up against so far this term." (Exeter Express and Echo)

OVF man of the match: Tom Pope

Post-match quote: "Port Vale are a very good side and they will be contenders (for promotion) this season." (Exeter boss Paul Tisdale)

However, there was some sad news on the 8th October when winger Lewis Haldane was forced to announce his retirement at just 27 years of age.

Haldane's injury hell

The winger had a luckless time at Vale Park. After a spell on loan, he signed a permanent deal in January 2010 and was then sent-off in his first game as a permanent Port Vale player.

In the summer of 2010 he was rushed to hospital after being bitten by an insect whilst training with the club. Haldane suffered blood poisoning and spent two weeks in hospital.

He recovered but in his first start following the bite he suffered a dreadful double fracture of his leg when landing awkwardly after heading the ball. Despite valiant attempts to recover from the injury, it proved to be too much and Haldane had to retire from the game.

Both of Haldane's former clubs rallied to his aid. Bristol Rovers organised a testimonial while Vale hosted a fundraising evening.

Another injury, this time a groin strain to goalkeeper Chris Neal meant that rookie Sam Johnson would make his debut in a game against Walsall. It turned out to be a memorable night for the young Vale goalkeeper.

Lewis Haldane was sadly forced to retire
[Photo: onevalefan.co.uk]

Match Fourteen
Opposition: Away to Walsall
Competition: Johnstone's Paints Trophy, round two
Date: October 9, 2012
Scoreline: Walsall 2-2 Port Vale (5-6 on pens)
Vale goals: Burge (49), Pope (61)
Attendance: 2,164 (943 away)

Pre-match quote: "Sam Johnson will start in goal, I think that will be his debut." (Micky Adams)

Port Vale line-up: Johnson, Yates, McCombe, Duffy (Davis), Taylor, Myrie-Williams, Burge, Shuker, Vincent (Lloyd) , Williamson (Dodds), Pope

Match report snippet: "Sam Johnson had a dream debut after he saved three penalties and scored the winner as Vale defeated local rivals Walsall in the JPT after a 22 player penalty shootout." (OVF)

OVF man of the match: Sam Johnson

Post-match quote: "I've never actually taken one [a penalty] before, so to score one on my debut, and for it to be the winner, is just incredible." (Sam Johnson)

"It's hard not to get carried away right now. It really is. I just can't help it."
– Columnist Martin Tideswell

The good news continued to flow at Vale Park. Following that dramatic win over local rivals Walsall in the cup, manager Micky Adams and striker Tom Pope were named September's nPower League Two manager and player of the month respectively.

"Micky's side have certainly impressed so far this season and recording 18 goals in just 6 games in September alone, makes this award truly deserving for Port Vale."
– nPower judging panel member Alan Curbishley, 12th October

"This has been a very difficult time for everyone at Port Vale and this is a nice reward for everyone who has worked hard for the good of the club, both on and off the pitch."
– Micky Adams, 13th October

By mid-October speculation was increasing over who would be the next preferred bidder and when it would be announced. On October 13th, local media claimed that an announcement was imminent and according to the Sentinel it was business duo Paul Wildes and Norman Smurthwaite who were set to get the nod from the club's administrators.

The deal was confirmed when Wildes issued a statement on the 15th October, which confirmed he was set to take over the club and that the deal would finally be announced on the 16th October.

Paul Wildes' statement, 15th October

"Alchemy Investment Group is an independent party, and to set the record straight we have no previous relationships with former employees, directors or shareholders at Port Vale, nor any other bidders.

"My passion is for competitive sport and my first priority is the supporters, who are the heart of this club. I want to pledge an ongoing commitment to keep supporters informed about decisions that affect their club. We plan to hold a fans forum over the next couple of weeks, and we look forward to hearing from supporters and discussing our plans with them.

"It is our intention to develop the club both on and off the field by improving the commercial side of the business and the match day experience. We also intend to develop the stadium and will be looking to make it a 7 day week venue.

"We are delighted to be on board and looking forward to the months and years ahead."

The new duo in charge

35 year-old Paul Wildes was born in Sheffield and had a range of business interests ranging from hairdressing to hotels. He had previously been close to acquiring control of Darlington.

52 year-old self-made millionaire Norman Smurthwaite was born and raised in Coventry and made his fortune through property development.

On the 16th October, Vale fans finally received the welcome news that Wildes and Smurthwaite were now the "preferred bidders" The sale price was £1.25m and the deal was set to be completed at the end of October. Head of Terms (i.e. the contract) had been signed and the Alchemy Group (the company set up to buy the club) had paid £100,000 for exclusivity.

"It's a sleeping giant, certainly at League Two level, and there is already a nice base to work on. But I can see big opportunities to do a lot more. I'm looking forward to it. It's going to be fun. We will own the stadium and we'll be debt-free, but we won't be pouring money into a black hole. We'll invest wisely, make sound commercial decisions and take long-term views."
- Paul Wildes, 16th October

"It's been an encouraging day. No-one is going to get carried away, of course, given what's happened previously. However, Mr Wildes said all the right things and everyone at the club – from the administrators to the staff and the manager all seemed very upbeat after their meetings with him."
– Supporters Club chairman Pete Williams on the announcement, 17th October

"I never quite got to the stage of hanging out the bunting and worshipping at the feet of Keith. Sadly, my caution over Ryder was born out by future events. It's for similar reasons, that I feel that "cautious optimism" should again be the reaction to the announcement that Paul Wildes is the club's preferred bidder...

That said, some fans will never be happy. If Robbie Williams took over the club, pledged £50m in transfer fees and personally scrubbed out the Railway toilets, he'd still be criticised for living in the USA, not being a proper fan or for his music becoming increasingly vapid."
– Rob Fielding blogs on the announcement, 17th October

"The new man appears to have a background which he's comfortable talking about – another reason for Vale supporters to perhaps have more confidence that this takeover may actually go through. Until the Football League are happy and until contracts are signed, however, no Vale fan can or should feel happy or content."
– Martin Tideswell on the announcement, 17th October

Meanwhile, back on the pitch, the Valiants were set to play a televised clash with Oxford United at Vale Park.

Match Fifteen
Opposition: Home to Oxford
Competition: League Two
Date: October 15, 2012
Scoreline: Port Vale 3-0 Oxford
Vale goals: Pope 30, Vincent 51, Morsy 61
Attendance: 4,596

Pre-match quote: "We'll be playing to a wider audience and we're looking forward to it. It's a chance for everyone to showcase themselves, both as individuals and as a team, and I'll be disappointed if we don't put on a show." (Micky Adams)

Port Vale line-up: Neal, Duffy (Yates), McCombe, Taylor, Myrie-Williams, Morsy, Burge (Shuker), Vincent, Dodds (Williamson), Pope

Match report snippet: "Micky Adams's men have not always fully fired at home this season but they were on course for victory once top scorer Tom Pope, who had already hit the bar, opened the scoring from close range. " (BBC)

OVF man of the match: Jennison Myrie-Williams

Post-match quote: "Our home form hasn't been great this season, so it was nice to send the fans home with a smile on their face. Our fitness levels are gaining us an extra five or 10 per cent on the other sides. When we've got five or six on their game, we can destroy teams and, at the moment, it's more like 10 or 11." (Tom Pope)

Match Sixteen
Opposition: Home to Wycombe
Competition: League Two
Date: October 20, 2012
Scoreline: Port Vale 4-1 Wycombe
Vale goals: Williamson (59), Pope (66, 87), Vincent (90)
Attendance: 5,305

Pre-match quote: "He's [Gareth Ainsworth] in charge in a caretaker capacity and I'd love him to get the job full-time, but I don't want him to get it because he gets a win at Vale Park. He's a friend of mine, but that will go right out of the window at 3 o'clock tomorrow." (Mark Grew)

Port Vale line-up: Neal, Duffy, McCombe, McDonald, Taylor, Myrie-Williams (Lloyd), Murphy (Williamson), Shuker (James), Vincent, Pope, Dodds

Match report snippet: "Striker Tom Pope made it fifteen goals for the season as Vale came from behind to beat ten man Wycombe at Vale Park." (BBC)

OVF man of the match: Tom Pope

Post-match quote:" I don't want to put a damper on it, but I was really disappointed with how we played in the first-half. We looked a tired and leggy unit and didn't do the right things. Our players were strutting around like peacocks and seemed to think they could just turn up and collect three points." (Micky Adams)

On the 22nd October, the Port Vale Supporters Club hailed two "very productive meetings with the new preferred bidders" and announced an email address through which fans can make suggestions for the potential owners.

However, on the pitch, suspensions and injuries were now taking their toll with defender Richard Duffy joining Clayton McDonald on the sidelines. At least the return of Ryan Burge to full fitness was giving Adams food for thought. The midfielder had missed most of last season through injury but was now fit and pushing for a place.

Meanwhile, the statue of Vale legend Roy Sproson was put in place in front of the main entrance to Vale Park ahead of its unveiling on the 17th November.

"There is still plenty of work to do before then and the statue has now been covered over again. We would like to take this opportunity to thank everyone who has played a part over the last 11 years in turning this tribute to the club's greatest servant into a reality."

– Supporters Club statement, 25th October

Match Seventeen
Opposition: Away to Burton
Competition: League Two
Date: October 23, 2012
Scoreline: Burton 1-1 Port Vale
Vale goals: Williamson (75)
Attendance: 3,975 (2,200 away)

Pre-match quote: "These derby games start fast and you want cool, calm heads in there – no rash tackles, no rash decisions and you have to see the game through." (Adam Yates)

Port Vale line-up: Neal, Duffy (Yates), McCombe, McDonald (Davis), Taylor, Myrie-Williams, Morsy, Shuker (Williamson) ,Vincent, Dodds , Pope

Match report snippet: "Port Vale failed to make it four straight wins in League Two but Ben Williamson stepped off the bench to salvage a point at Burton." (BBC)

OVF man of the match: Clayton McDonald

Post-match quote: "The squad is stretched now, but there's nothing we can do. We'll just have to get on with it. "(Micky Adams)

Match Eighteen
Opposition: Away to Northampton
Competition: League Two
Date: October 27, 2012
Scoreline: Northampton 2-0 Port Vale
Vale goals: none
Attendance: 5,061 (994 away)

Pre-match quote: "We've had injury and suspension in defence and there's a chance now for the players that have been patient on the bench." (Micky Adams)

Port Vale line-up: Neal, Yates, McCombe, Owen (James), Taylor, Myrie-Williams, Morsy (Lloyd), Burge, Vincent, Williamson (Davis), Pope

Match report snippet: "Vale were left with a depleted defence for their opening FA Cup tie with Forest Green after John McCombe was sent-off and Gareth Owen was injured during the 2-0 defeat to Northampton.." (OVF)

OVF man of the match: Ryan Burge

Post-match quote: "All my thoughts are with Alex Nicholls [who broke his leg after a tackle by John McCombe] at the moment and everyone connected with Port Vale wishes Alex a speedy recovery. But I've just seen the tackle and it's a genuine attempt by John [McCombe] to win the ball and it's an unfortunate accident. John is distraught about it." (Micky Adams)

Despite the Northampton defeat, John McCombe's red card and the shock of Alex Nicholls' broken leg, Vale's future both on and off the pitch were looking healthier.

The Valiants were still in second place and by now, decent contenders for promotion to League One. Tom Pope was continuing to find the back of the net. The long-awaited Sproson statue was set to be unveiled. And perhaps most importantly of all new, progressive and forward-thinking owners were all set to take over.

Much credit for the improved off-pitch state of affairs had to go to the Port Vale Supporters Club who had kept fans informed, rallied volunteers to help the club and generally fought tooth and nail to keep Port Vale alive.

The Supporters Club, in conjunction with the administrators (who had done a better job than two previous boards) and with the backing of Stoke-on-Trent council had done enough to give Vale a fighting chance of surviving.

As long as they didn't do a Ryder-esque disappearing act, the preferred bidders were saying all the right things and although fans were understandably cautious, the future looked bright.

And with Micky Adams working miracles on the pitch, there was even a chance of the club winning promotion, something that had appeared nearly impossible at the start of the campaign.

Manager Micky Adams had guided Vale to second place in the League Two table by the end of October [Photo: onevalefan.co.uk]

League Two table: end of October

	Club	GD	Points
1	Gillingham	+20	35
2	**Port Vale**	**+17**	**30**
3	Cheltenham	+5	28
4	Fleetwood	+8	26
5	Bradford City	+6	24

November: Roy, Rovers and revival

"In the light of confirmation of the Football League's approval for a takeover by Paul Wildes and Norman Smurthwaite, the Supporters' Club would like to thank everyone who helped to rescue Port Vale from a self-interested few."

– Supporters Club statement, 20th November

Match Nineteen
Opposition: Away to Forest Green Rovers
Competition: FA Cup, round one
Date: November 3, 2012
Scoreline: Forest Green 2-3 Port Vale
Vale goals: Vincent (6), McDonald (12), Williamson (85)
Attendance: 1,753 (792 away)

Pre-match quote: "They'll be really up for it and will try to press us, so we have to match them in that respect. Their players will be looking forward to having a crack at League Two guys." (Tom Pope)

Port Vale line-up: Neal, Yates, McDonald, Davis, Taylor (Loft), Myrie-Williams (Shuker), Morsy, Burge, Vincent, Dodds (Williamson), Pope

Match report snippet: "Substitute Ben Williamson broke Forest Green hearts as his late winner saw Port Vale edge home at The New Lawn." (BBC)

OVF man of the match: Clayton McDonald

Post-match quote: "I think if anyone thought we could come here and put them on their backs and tickle their bellies they were sadly wrong. It was never going to be easy." (Micky Adams)

A TV cameraman at the Forest Green Rovers game (above), the
Forest Green mascot (below left) and expectant Port Vale fans
(below right) [Photos: Pete Tindall]

The month started on a bright note with the news that Ashley Vincent was the League Two player of the month for October while the Valiants had been rewarded for their victory over Forest Green with a second-round tie against Sheffield United, manager Micky Adams' boyhood idols.

Following the sterling work by the Supporters Club to keep the Vale alive during the dark days, there was sad news on the 4th October with the announcement that Chairman Pete Williams had suffered a stroke. Hundreds of fans sent get well messages to Williams, who had been admitted to hospital.

Paul Wildes issued another statement informing fans that he expects the "takeover will be completed within the next 10-15 days." Fans, who had heard similar statements from Keith Ryder were understandably cautious – many would not accept a deal was done until Wildes and Smurthwaite were confirmed as the club's new owners by the Football League.

Match Twenty
Opposition: At home to Rochdale
Competition: League Two
Date: November 6, 2012
Scoreline: Port Vale 2-2 Rochdale
Vale goals: Pope (30, 60)
Attendance: 4,139

Pre-match quote: "We are getting goals from all areas, we're not relying on goals from Tom Pope, as we proved on Saturday, and we will continue in the same vein." (Micky Adams)

Port Vale line-up: Neal, Yates, Davis, McDonald, Loft (Taylor), Myrie-Williams, Morsy, Burge, Vincent, Pope, Williamson (Murphy (James))

Match report snippet: "The game changed when Vale were reduced to 10 men as Sam Morsy was red-carded for a late tackle." (BBC)

OVF man of the match: Tom Pope

Post-match quote: "I will be honest. I called Sam a coward after the game. He went for the ball, but he also then went to hurt their lad. I don't want to see that in my team." (Micky Adams)

Sam Morsy's red card and subsequent suspension wasn't the only blow for the Valiants. Captain Doug Loft was unable to complete the game, while substitute Darren Murphy had also been injured and had to be replaced just minutes after taking to the field.

The injuries and suspensions left Vale short of numbers for the trip to Southend with just 15 players available for selection. On the 8th November, manager Micky Adams told the official Port Vale website that the club's administrators have spoken to the Football League about getting special dispensation to bring in a player on loan.

The next day, trialist Sean McAllister, who had been training with the club was allowed to sign for the Valiants on a two month deal. Following the retirement of Lewis Haldane in October, the club's administrators were able to successfully argue that there had been a need to add an additional player to the ranks.

On the same day, there was more positive news about the Wildes-Smurthwaite takeover. The Supporters Club had reported "further talks" with Norman Smurthwaite and the preferred bidders were now confident of completing their deal before the 20th November.

"Mr Smurthwaite said he was spending a great deal of time at Vale Park and had been chuffed to receive two, hand-made scarves from Vale supporter Sheila Wilkie which he will treasure."

– Supporters Club statement, 9th November.

Match Twenty One
Opposition: Away to Southend
Competition: League Two
Date: November 10, 2012
Scoreline: Southend 0-0 Port Vale
Vale goals: none
Attendance: 4,876 (182 away)

Pre-match quote: "Can we use a baseball bat?"
(Southend boss Paul Sturrock on how to control Vale's
Tom Pope)

Port Vale line-up: Neal, Yates, McDonald, Davis, Taylor,
Myrie-Williams (Duffy), Dodds, Burge, Vincent, Pope,
Williamson (Shuker)

Match report snippet: "The Valiants earnt a valuable
away point against Southend after securing a goalless
draw at Roots Hall." (OVF)

OVF man of the match: Chris Neal

Post-match quote: "Both keepers were outstanding and
made some great saves." (Micky Adams)

Following earlier criticism by Micky Adams, midfielder Sam Morsy issued a public apology for the tackle which saw him red-carded against Rochdale.

'This season has been a huge learning curve in my development as a player and I can only apologise that my sending off affected the result last Tuesday. There is no-one more disappointed with that than me."

- Sam Morsy, 12th November

And as preparations began in earnest for the unveiling of the Roy Sproson statue ahead of the club's next game, a host of initiatives were announced. Limited edition tankards were to go on sale and a minute's applause was announced – it was planned to take place eight minutes, 37 seconds into the game against York City – which would mark Sproson's 837 starts for the club.

To complete a busy week, the club announced that a shirt sponsorship had been agreed with local firm UK Windows System with the deal in place for the rest of the season.

Sam Morsy: on a learning curve [Photo: onevalefan.co.uk]

Roy returns home

The sixteen-foot tall statue of Roy Sproson was unveiled before the York City game on the 17th November with over a thousand Vale fans, dignitaries and the Sproson family watching on.

Here is a selection of quotes from a memorable day:

'The statue will be a constant reminder of Roy's efforts for this club. He's an iconic figure and an inspiration too."
- Mohammed Pervez, Stoke-on-Trent City Council leader

"It's a great tribute to a unique footballing family."
– Gordon Taylor, Chairman of the PFA

"Roy was a fantastic player and a fantastic man. His family is all about the club and you've got to admire them."
- former team-mate Colin Askey

"I'd like to pay tribute to the people who made this happen, those who love Vale and who've never given up."
- MP Joan Whalley

The unveiling of the Roy Sproson statue [Photo: AS Photos]

Match Twenty Two
Opposition: Home to York
Competition: League Two
Date: November 17, 2012
Scoreline: Port Vale 2-2 York City
Vale goals: Burge (30), Myrie-Williams (44, pen)
Attendance: 5,380

Pre-match quote: "They are going to cause us real problems and we have got to be on our game to combat their strengths." (Micky Adams)

Port Vale line-up: Neal, Duffy, McCombe, McDonald, Yates, Myrie-Williams, Burge, Shuker (Williamson), Taylor (McAllister), Pope, Dodds

Match report snippet: "Goals from Ryan Burge and Jennison Myrie-Williams were cancelled out by strikes for Rodman and Reid as Vale threw away a two goal lead at home." (OVF)

OVF man of the match: Ryan Burge

Post-match quote: "We were the better team today and to go in 2-0 down was a travesty to be honest." (York boss Gary Mills)

With the Wildes-Smurthwaite duo extremely confident of completing their takeover later that day, on the 20th November, manager Micky Adams was keen to strengthen his squad ahead of the Thursday 22nd loan deadline.

'The gaffer has been given the go-ahead to bring in fresh faces once the takeover is completed and he's told the players that, so there could well be new arrivals."

– Mark Grew, 20th November

And lo and behold, at 4pm on the 20th November, less than four hours before the home game with Bristol Rovers, Port Vale's 252 day spell in administration finally came to an end as the club announced that the Wildes-Smurthwaite takeover had been approved and the Football League had transferred its all-important "golden share".

The city council, which had bankrolled Port Vale's administration and who had lent the former board £2.3m would receive £740,000 back from the new owners.

Wildes and his business partner Norman Smurthwaite were given a standing ovation by fans attending the Bristol Rovers game.

"Having worked at Vale Park on a daily basis over the last few weeks, I fully recognise the potential of the Club and feel truly excited about what we can achieve."

- Norman Smurthwaite, 20th November

"Myself and Norman are looking forward to 10, 15, 20 years taking Port Vale back to where it should be."

– Paul Wildes, 20th November

The takeover – reaction ...

"In the light of confirmation of the Football League's approval for a takeover by Paul Wildes and Norman Smurthwaite, the Supporters' Club would like to thank everyone who helped to rescue Port Vale from a self-interested few and given fans hope for the future."

– Supporters Club statement

"We are pleased to pass the baton on to Paul and Norman and we wish them all the very best for the future. We are proud of our role in saving Port Vale and we will continue with our investigation work into antecedent transactions, in particular the issuing of nil paid shares."

– Bob Young

"I say 'well done' to all of those who stood up, said 'enough is enough' and decided to take action to make Vale's future brighter. You should all be proud of yourselves today."

– Rob Fielding on his OVF blog

Chairman Paul Wildes [Photo: Pete Tindall]

CEO Norman Smurthwaite [Photo: Pete Tindall]

Match Twenty Three
Opposition: At home to Bristol Rovers
Date: November 20, 2012
Scoreline: Port Vale 4-0 Bristol Rovers
Vale goals: Pope (20, 22, 67), Williamson (35)
Attendance: 4,177

Pre-match quote: "We might well have to be patient. I think Bristol will come here looking for a draw like a lot of teams have. So we have to cut out the lapses at the back and keep our concentration." (Mark Grew)

Port Vale line-up: Neal, Duffy, McCombe, McDonald (Davis), Yates, Myrie-Williams, Burge (McAllister), James, Vincent, Pope (Lloyd), Williamson

Match report snippet: "Tom Pope became the fastest player to score twenty goals in the club's history as the Valiants celebrated the Paul Wildes takeover with a comprehensive thrashing of Bristol Rovers." (OVF)

OVF man of the match: Tom Pope

Post-match quote: "Now Paul and Norman have come in we can make one or two additions to our playing squad. We've got two days to bring in loan players. Some clubs have much larger squads than we have, but that just leaves the manager with problems, I don't like problems, I like a nice dressing room with everybody singing from the same hymn sheet." (Micky Adams)

As Tom Pope continued to score with abandon, it was no surprise when the club were reported to have offered him a contract extension.

After a poor goalscoring return the previous season, Pope had only been offered a one-year deal, but with the striker already on twenty goals in mid-November, the club was rightly keen to keep hold of their talisman.

Meanwhile, with the loan deadline on Thursday the 24th November, attention now turned to which players Micky Adams would attempt to bring in the strengthen his squad. The transfer embargo, which had been in force throughout the club's time in administration had been lifted following the takeover and Adams was now free to undertake a little 'shopping.'

"I will be working with Micky [Adams] over the next forty eight hours to add players to his squad that he wants to bring in."

– Paul Wildes, 22nd October

After all the crisis and drama of the spell in administration, surely the club's move into the transfer market should be a relatively easy affair? However, as with most things that happened during this remarkable season, it turned out to be a drama all of its very own.

Deadline day debacle

A day that should have seen Micky Adams sign three players, ended with just one joining as Vale suffered more embarrassment.

By mid-afternoon on deadline day, the rumour mill was in full swing and Nottingham newspapers were claiming that Vale were signing striker Lee Hughes from Notts County.

But by late evening, there was no official confirmation of the Hughes switch on the official Port Vale website, only the signing of defender Liam Chilvers was confirmed.

What happened the next day, heaped considerable embarrassment onto the club.

Notts County issued a statement claiming that "paperwork did not go through in time" to meet the Football League deadline. Vale appealed to the League to ratify the move (and a bid for another, unnamed player) but the League confirmed that the moves had been blocked as they were submitted too late.

It was a thoroughly embarrassing day for the Vale. It was hardly a last-minute move, Hughes had been at the club for most of the day, and the deadline of 5pm was public knowledge.

Now, Micky Adams would have to soldier on until the January transfer window.

Match Twenty Four
Opposition: Away to Aldershot
Competition: League Two
Date: November 24, 2012
Scoreline: Aldershot 1-3 Port Vale
Vale goals: Williamson(17), Burge (47), Myrie-Williams (76, pen)
Attendance: 1,992 (239 away)

Pre-match quote: "They'll be fighting for a result and it will be another tough game for us. They want the three points as much as we do." (Ben Williamson)

Port Vale line-up: Neal, Duffy, McDonald (Chilvers), McCombe, Yates, Vincent, Burge, James, Myrie-Williams (Shuker), Williamson (Dodds), Pope

Match report snippet: "Port Vale extended their unbeaten run to six games with a win at Aldershot, who slipped back into the bottom two." (BBC)

OVF man of the match: Ryan Burge

Post-match quote: "It's been a good week. I took my daughter up the aisle and we've come away with the win." (Micky Adams)

Vale flags at the Aldershot game [Photos: Pete Tindall]

Following the club's failure in the loan market, the Valiants announced that free agent Calvin Andrew, a powerful forward, had agreed a short-term contract with the club. Meanwhile, former midfielder Chris Birchall, another free agent after leaving Colombus Crew, was training with the side.

During a well-attended fans forum, the new owners outlined their plans for the club. Wildes and Smurthwaite received a standing ovation from those present as they explained their goal of placing the Valiants at the heart of the community.

"We'll be launching a Young Supporters' club, we'll re-engage local schools, we're bringing in an academy and we're very keen to inspire a generation of people to want to come and support Port Vale. We want to place the club back in the heart of the area – that's what the business strategy is all about."
– Paul Wildes, 29th November

In many ways, November was the turning point of the season for the Valiants. The new owners had so far turned out to be a breath of fresh air and in the space of a few weeks had been more progressive and unifying than the previous two regimes put together.

The unveiling of the Roy Sproson statue had also been a unifying moment. Even though there had been an embarrassing transfer window debacle, it still hadn't dampened the air of optimism around Vale Park and fans would be hoping for more positive news before the season was out because on the pitch Port Vale were still on course to go up...

League Two table: end of November

	Club	GD	Points
1	Gillingham	+20	41
2	**Port Vale**	**+23**	**39**
3	Cheltenham	+2	35
4	Rotherham	+4	34
5	Southend Utd	+12	32

December: ending the year on a high

"I'd like to thank our fans for their support during the first part of the season, I want them to enjoy where we are, and I want them to keep backing us all the way."
– Micky Adams, 29th December

Match Twenty Five
Opposition: Away to Sheffield United
Competition: FA Cup, round two
Date: December 1, 2012
Scoreline: Sheffield Utd 2-1 Port Vale
Vale goals: Pope (33)
Attendance: 10,215 (3,295 away)

Pre-match quote: "I'm not sure how it will feel to go back. I've focused this week on preparing the team and making sure they're right and not thought about me, but it will be special for me and my family." (Micky Adams)

Port Vale line-up: Neal, Duffy, McDonald, McCombe, Yates, Myrie-Williams (Dodds), Burge, James, Vincent (Taylor), Pope, Williamson (Andrew)

Match report snippet: "Trailing to Tom Pope's first-half strike, the League One club appeared to be heading out of the competition at the second-round stage until two late goals from Shaun Miller wrecked Port Vale's hopes of causing an upset." (Sheffield Star)

OVF man of the match: Chris Neal

Post-match quote: "We couldn't see the job through but I'm proud of the lads." (Micky Adams)

There was sad news on the 2nd December after it was announced that former Vale favourite Steve Fox had passed away at the weekend. It had been revealed earlier in the year that Fox, who helped Vale to promotion in 1983, was suffering from a rare form of cancer. As Fox's condition worsened, messages of support from Vale fans had been passed onto the Fox family by OVF earlier in the week. Steve had thanked the Vale fans for their "kind words" before sadly passing away two days later.

'The Fox family are very much in my thoughts right now. Steve's memory will live on at Vale Park and his contribution to the 1982-83 promotion season will not be forgotten by an older generation of Port Vale fans."

– Rob Fielding, 2nd December

In midweek, the Vale would be in action in the Johnstone's Paints Trophy, the sole cup competition in which they had an interest. By this stage of the season injuries and suspensions were starting to hurt Vale's small squad and Tom Pope, Ryan Burge and Richard Duffy would all miss the match through suspension.

Match Twenty Six
Opposition: At home to Bradford City
Competition: Johnstone's Paints Trophy Northern QF
Date: December 4, 2012
Scoreline: Port Vale 0-2 Bradford City
Vale goals: none
Attendance: 2,786

Pre-match quote: "Keeping him [Tom Pope] in check is a good challenge for our back four but one we're looking forward to." (Bradford boss Phil Parkinson was unaware that Pope was, in fact, suspended)

Port Vale line-up: Neal, Yates, McCombe, Chilvers, Loft, Myrie-Williams, Morsy, McAllister (Shuker), Vincent, Williamson (Dodds), Andrew (Taylor)

Match report snippet: "The Valiants exited their second cup campaign of the week after they lost their Johnstone's Paints Northern Area Quarter Final game against Bradford City." (OVF)

OVF man of the match: Adam Yates

Post-match quote: "We were poor individually and collectively. I'm disappointed we've gone out and we've done so in a fashion that doesn't please me." (Micky Adams)

Match Twenty Seven
Opposition: At home to Chesterfield
Competition: League Two
Date: December 8, 2012
Scoreline: Port Vale 0-2 Chesterfield
Vale goals: none
Attendance: 5,298

Pre-match quote: "They are a threat, but we won't worry ourselves about their individuals or them as a unit. The onus will be on us to entertain and get three points." (Micky Adams)

Port Vale line-up: Neal, Duffy, McCombe, McDonald, Loft (Dodds), Myrie-Williams, Burge, James (Taylor), Vincent, Pope, Andrew (Shuker)

Match report snippet: "Jay O'Shea scored against his former club as Chesterfield extended their winning run to four league games with victory at promotion-chasing Port Vale." (BBC)

OVF man of the match: Chris Neal

Post-match quote: "There's no panic and no crisis, certainly not in our own minds, but we need the bigger players to come alive again and show everybody what they're capable of doing." (Micky Adams)

Port Vale co-owner Norman Smurthwaite made headlines in hometown Coventry on the 14th December as he offered a lifeline to the financially troubled League One outfit who were in dispute with their stadium owners over an unpaid rent bill.

"If City end up needing a stadium, I'd be prepared to do a ground share. They haven't asked, but I'd to do it until the end of this season, though I wouldn't do it next season because we'll be playing them in League One. We certainly wouldn't let them come for free. But I would enter dialogue with them."

– Norman Smurthwaite, 14th December

Meanwhile, Chairman of the Supporters Club, Pete Williams, told the *Sentinel* that Vale fans will always remember the financial support of Stoke-on-Trent city council. The council, which was Vale's biggest creditor at the time of the crisis, placed the club into administration in March to help secure its future in the wake of a winding up order for unpaid taxes.

"Port Vale supporters will be forever thankful to the city council for what they've done in helping to save the club. I feel they've recognised that if the club disappeared we would also be losing peoples' jobs and an important part of Burslem. It would have been a tremendous loss. The importance of the club surviving is not something you can put a price on."

– Pete Williams, 15th December

Match Twenty Eight
Opposition: Away to Cheltenham
Competition: League Two
Date: December 15, 2012
Scoreline: Cheltenham 1-1 Port Vale
Vale goals: Dodds (67)
Attendance: 3,670 (331 away)

Pre-match quote: "It'll be strange coming back to play against Cheltenham because when I was younger I used to watch them every week. I know so many people in the town and a lot of my mates are fans." (Ryan Burge)

Port Vale line-up: Neal, Duffy, McCombe, Chilvers, Loft, Vincent (Williamson), Morsy, Burge, Taylor (Shuker), Pope, Dodds (Andrew)

Match report snippet: "Louis Dodds ended his fifteen game goal drought to score his fifth of the season as Vale picked up an away point against Cheltenham Town." (OVF)

OVF man of the match: Louis Dodds

Post-match quote: "I was left scratching my head a little bit with him [Dodds]. I've put him back in there and he has worked hard for the team but also he's got his goal which will hopefully kickstart him." (Micky Adams)

The Valiants' winless run on the pitch now stretched to four games and Micky Adams was keen to appeal for patience from the Vale support, which was growing restless.

"We sometimes get nervous and the crowd gets nervous. It's a lesson for our crowd to just stay patient with what we're trying to do at home because nerves do set in. If we don't score in the first 20 minutes, it seems to be a crisis. But we just have to work out ways to be better."

– Micky Adams, 17th December

There was a further appeal to fans, this time from co-owner Norman Smurthwaite who wanted to see attendances increase at Vale Park.

"History shows the club had a larger fan base in years gone by, and they haven't all died or moved away. If supporters want to stay in League Two, then 5,000 crowds will deliver League Two football. If we do get promoted, we'll be keen to give Micky Adams the ability to strengthen the squad, but it depends on supporters."

– Norman Smurthwaite, 20th December

However, Smurthwaite's wish to see more fans at Vale Park was to suffer early disappointment as their next fixture, a home game against AFC Wimbledon, was called off due to a waterlogged pitch.

The Valiants' final games of the year would be the Boxing Day fixture against promotion rivals Rotherham, followed by a trip to Dagenham, three days later.

Match Twenty Nine
Opposition: Away to Rotherham
Competition: League Two
Date: December 26, 2012
Scoreline: Rotherham 1-2 Port Vale
Vale goals: Dodds (55), Pope (62)
Attendance: 10,502 (1,352 away)

Pre-match quote: "As a game it is not the be-all and end-all of the season if we lose or win because there are still an awful lot of games to go. But it will be a big game, no doubt about it." (Mark Grew)

Port Vale line-up: Neal, Duffy, Chilvers, McCombe, Yates, Loft, Morsy, Burge, Myrie-Williams (Taylor), Pope, Dodds (Andrew)

Match report snippet: "From Vale's viewpoint it was a classic away performance of its kind in that they defended in numbers, put bodies on the line defensively, worked like dervishes all over the pitch and then made the most of the rare moments of real threat." (Sheffield Star)

OVF man of the match: Ryan Burge

Post-match quote: "Our results so far speak for themselves. We are up there to be shot at. We have just got to concentrate on ourselves and prepare for games and the effort and enthusiasm they have shown today will carry them a long way." (Micky Adams)

Match Thirty
Opposition: Away to Dagenham
Competition: League Two
Date: December 29, 2012
Scoreline: Dagenham 2-3 Port Vale
Vale goals: Pope (4), Myrie-Williams (9), Dodds (39)
Attendance: 1,697 (256 away)

Pre-match quote: "I've not had an easy game yet in League Two and I'm certainly not expecting one at Dagenham." (Micky Adams)

Port Vale line-up: Neal, Duffy, McCombe, Chilvers, Yates, Myrie-Williams (Taylor), Morsy, Burge, Dodds (McDonald), Pope, Andrew

Match report snippet: "Port Vale moved to the top of League Two with a win at Dagenham & Redbridge. Gillingham had been top of the table since the start of September but Vale were handed the chance to leapfrog them after the Gills' game at home to Northampton was postponed." (BBC)

OVF man of the match: Louis Dodds

Post-match quote: "Louis Dodds looks rejuvenated at the moment. He looks a confident boy, and that's not any credit to me, that's down to him." (Micky Adams)

Despite all the problems in the summer, and against all the pre-season odds, with that victory over Dagenham Micky Adams' Port Vale FC had finished 2012 on top of the League Two table.

After the chaos surrounding the start of the season, it was an incredible achievement and manager Adams deserved much praise for how he had managed to keep players focussed on the job at hand amid confusion and crisis off it.

Nevertheless, it was merely the half-way stage of the season. Expectations had been raised following the Wildes-Smurthwaite takeover, could the club continue their form in 2013 and establish themselves as genuine promotion contenders? There was still work to be done...

League Two Table: end of December

	Club	GD	Points
1	**Port Vale**	**+23**	**46**
2	Gillingham	+20	45
3	Cheltenham	+4	42
4	Southend Utd	+16	40
5	Rotherham	+6	40

January: new year, new additions

"The fans can rest assured that there will be four or five new faces coming into the club."

– Micky Adams, 3rd January

With new owners in place, the Valiants were now free of their transfer embargo and were able to use the January transfer window to bring in new recruits to strengthen their small squad (providing they didn't miss any deadlines this time around!). However, Micky Adams also suggested that some players who were not being picked regularly may move on first.

"I don't expect players not on the fringes of the team to be happy so there could be a couple on their way out."
– Micky Adams, 1st January

And later that same day, Sean McAllister, who had struggled to break through into the first-team since his short-term deal was released with the club's best wishes.

"It's unfortunate that we weren't able to offer Sean more first-team opportunities but that underlines the competition for places we have among the squad."
– Micky Adams, 1st January

Match Thirty One
Opposition: Home to Fleetwood
Competition: League Two
Date: January 1, 2013
Scoreline: Port Vale 0-2 Fleetwood
Vale goals: none
Attendance: 6,082

Pre-match quote: "It's going to be a hard game against Fleetwood, but with the two wins we've got at Christmas, we'll go in against them confident." (Calvin Andrew)

Port Vale line-up: Neal, Duffy (Taylor), McCombe (McDonald), Chilvers, Yates, Myrie-Williams, Morsy, Burge, Andrew (Vincent), Pope, Dodds

Match report snippet: "Goals from David Ball and Alan Goodall helped Fleetwood Town to a shock victory at Vale Park. Vale tried their best to strike back and won a penalty midway through the second half, Scott Davies saving the spot kick." (Blackpool Gazette)

OVF man of the match: Sam Morsy

Post-match quote: "Everybody's getting excited about the transfer window, but we'll take a rational decision about everything once the emotion of this game has gone and we can think a bit clearer. At this moment, do I want to bring any players in? Yes, of course I do. But that's me when we've lost a game." (Micky Adams)

Despite the disappointment of the Fleetwood defeat, Vale didn't want to rush their recruitment drive and in his post-match press conference, Micky Adams admitted that he still hadn't had a conversation about new recruits with the club's new owners.

"We'll sit down and analyse what we've done so far, assess all areas of the squad and then decide what we want to do. I haven't had that conversation yet with Paul [Wildes] and Norman [Smurthwaite]."

- Micky Adams, 2nd January

One player who appeared to have ruled himself out was November target Lee Hughes. Notts County player Hughes had told local newspapers in Nottingham that "I 100 per cent want to be here. " It seemed unlikely that Vale would revive their interest in the veteran striker.

Meanwhile, Vale were fending off interest in their own players with Peterborough United rumoured to be interested in the now prolific forward Tom Pope.

However, no bids for Vale players materialized and it was Vale who acted to strengthen their squad. In the modern, Internet age, it was perhaps no surprise that the first signing for the Wildes-Smurthwaite partnership was first announced via social media.

On the 3rd January, tweets from former Valiant Chris Birchall and chairman Paul Wildes confirmed that the former midfielder had rejoined Vale for a second spell.

"Delighted to secure Chris Birchall until the end of the campaign - I know most Vale fans remember him fondly from his time here previously."
– a tweet from Chairman Paul Wildes, 3rd January

Following that signing was the confirmation by Micky Adams that more signings would be on their way.

Chris Birchall, who had played for the club between 2001 and 2006 rejoined for a second spell at Vale Park [Photo: onevalefan.co.uk]

"In the cold light of day, I think we need additions to the squad and I have had some great conversations with the owners of the football club and we are all in agreement that we will add new faces to the squad. We have a list of players and I will be sitting down with the staff and Paul Wildes and Norman Smurthwaite, but we are well down the road in terms of signing a couple of players. The fans can rest assured that there will be four or five new faces coming in to the club."

– Micky Adams, 3rd January

The club's rapid adoption of social media as its preferred method of breaking news continued apace as another new signing was announced by the Chairman. This time, the player would be confirmed on Saturday with the rumourmill speculating it was Darren Purse, ironically part of Plymouth's squad who were set to visit Burslem.

"Looking forward to the game tomorrow and finalising another transfer which we will announce at half time!"

– a tweet by Paul Wildes, 5th January

Match Thirty Two
Opposition: Home to Plymouth
Competition: League Two
Date: January 5, 2013
Scoreline: Port Vale 4-0 Plymouth
Vale goals: Myrie-Williams (32), Pope (55, 83), Williamson (77)
Attendance: 5,139

Pre-match quote: "Confidence is a fragile thing in footballers so we have got to try and capitalise on their uncertainty and get back to winning ways and I have got every confidence that you will see a different side on Saturday." (Micky Adams)

Port Vale line-up: Neal, Yates, Chilvers, Davis, Taylor, Myrie-Williams (Birchall), Loft, Shuker, Vincent (Lloyd), Pope, Williamson (Andrew)

Match report snippet: "Tom Pope made it 25 goals for the season as Vale brushed aside ten man Plymouth 4-0 at Vale Park." (OVF)

OVF man of the match: Ben Williamson

Post-match quote: "I defy anyone not to pass judgement on that idiot who got sent off [Plymouth's Nick Chadwick]. What a stupid boy he is. He could have got sent off in the first minute. That elbow was worse than the second one he got done for. He's obviously not the brightest." (Micky Adams)

During the game against Plymouth, Vale had indeed confirmed the signing of veteran defender Purse, who had not been included in the Plymouth matchday squad.

By now, speculation amongst Vale fans was reaching fever pitch and a further tweet by chairman Wildes increased the excitement still further.

"Spent the day negotiating another signing and I am pleased to confirm we are all agreed. We will announce the player Tuesday #bigsigning"
– a tweet by chairman Paul Wildes, 7th January

However, manager Micky Adams was quick to down play Wildes' tweet.

"I haven't seen the Twitter feed, if that's the right word, that the chairman sends out. We are negotiating with a player at the moment and hopefully that will be sorted out sooner rather than later. As I've said many times, until the body is in the building and signed the papers I won't speculate."

– Micky Adams, 7th January

The following day, January 8th was a busy one for the club as firstly, defender Gareth Owen and midfielder Darren Murphy, who had both been hampered by injury all season left the club by mutual consent. And at lunchtime, Vale confirmed that their 'big signing' was indeed Lee Hughes, who despite his earlier comments about wanting to stay at Notts County had instead joined Vale on a permanent deal.

The signing received a mixed reception from fans with some supporters unhappy that Vale had signed a player with Hughes' chequered history, whilst others welcomed a proven and experienced goalscorer to the club.

"I am really looking forward to working with Micky Adams, who I have long respected. The team is having a tremendous season and so I shall do my utmost to score goals and help the team in its promotion push."
– Lee Hughes, 8th January

It was a hectic day for the Valiants and the Hughes signing would prove to be a crucial one for the club's promotion hopes. What's more, it was revealed that Hughes had turned down promotion rivals Gillingham when deciding to join Micky Adams' side.

Vale were delighted to sign veteran striker Lee Hughes after a protracted chase for the forward [Photo: Pete Tindall]

Vale's signing spree seemed unlikely to end just yet as the club was also linked with a possible move for a left-back.

In what was turning out to be a busy month for the new owners, on the 10th January the club announced that it wanted to introduce a new crest for the next season. The crest, which was a design based upon the club's 1954 effort included the strap line "For all who have gone before" and fans were asked to vote on the new design.

"We want to recognise the history and heritage of supporters and players alike who have helped to shape the club today and embrace this as part of our future. We believe that reintroducing a former crest for next season, along with a strap line which recognises all who have played their own unique part, will help to do this."
- Club statement, 10th January

The proposed club crest

After all the excitement on the pitch, it was now time for Vale to travel to promotion rivals Gillingham for a crucial League Two encounter.

Match Thirty Three
Opposition: Away to Gillingham
Competition: League Two
Date: January 12, 2013
Scoreline: Gillingham 1-2 Port Vale
Vale goals: Hughes (38), Pope (83)
Attendance: 8,392 (716 away)

Pre-match quote: "We now have good options and can use different styles. We've got a real mixture there, particularly in terms of front play. We can mix it at any given moment against any given team." (Micky Adams)

Port Vale line-up: Neal, Duffy, Chilvers, Purse, Yates, Myrie-Williams (Andrew), Burge, Loft, Vincent (Taylor), Pope, Hughes (Williamson)

Match report snippet: "A smash and grab performance from Port Vale sent them top of League Two despite Gillingham giving all they could in an entertaining game. Martin Allen's side were undone by a resolute Vale side that got in front and despite conceding straight away, held on to go a point clear at the top of the table." (Kent Sports News)

OVF man of the match: Darren Purse

Post-match quote: "Racing into a two-goal lead, it looked as though we were comfortable at that stage but Gillingham don't give you a minute's peace, you can see why they've been top of the table for so long. It feels great being top. It's doubly hard now - we're there to be shot at." (Micky Adams)

With several new signings on the books and a win over their nearest rivals, it's fair to say that things were looking good at Vale Park. But one thing the new owners could not defeat was the awful weather sweeping the United Kingdom at the start of the year.

On the 18th January, the club appealed for volunteers to try and ensure that the home game against Bradford went ahead. The club even used industrial dryers that had been provided by a local firm, but it was all to no avail as the game was called off due to a frozen pitch.

Another new face arrived at the club on the 21st January as tall left-back Dan Jones joined until the end of the season. Meanwhile, central defender Clayton McDonald was loaned out to Bristol Rovers.

However, the weather was still hampering Vale's attempts to play football with opponents Wimbledon appealing for volunteers to ensure their televised game against Vale went ahead.

With so much bad weather across the country, keeping the players match fit was a concern. So the club's owners announced that the team would train on the all-weather facilities enjoyed by the England national team after the club had agreed a short-term contract to use the St George's Park facilities in nearby Burton. It was a sign of how much the club had changed under the new owners.

Luckily, the weather eased off enough for the Wimbledon game to take place.

Match Thirty Four
Opposition: Away to Wimbledon
Competition: League Two
Date: January 24, 2013
Scoreline: Wimbledon 2-2 Port Vale
Vale goals: Jones (44), Pope (58)
Attendance: 3,395 (208 away)

Pre-match quote: "There will be a live TV audience so once again it's a chance to showcase ourselves as a football club and as a team. It's a chance for the players to showcase themselves as individuals and we are looking forward to the game." (Micky Adams)

Port Vale line-up: Neal, Duffy, Chilvers, Purse, Jones, Myrie-Williams, Burge, Loft (Morsy), Vincent (Andrew), Pope, Hughes (Williamson)

Match report snippet: "Tom Pope's second-half strike salvaged a point for League Two leaders Port Vale as they drew 2-2 at struggling AFC Wimbledon." (Sporting Life)

OVF man of the match: Dan Jones

Post-match quote: "Every point is important. Who is to say that won't make a difference come the end of the season, I'm not Mystic Meg." (Micky Adams)

The month continued to be one of comings and goings as young midfielder Kingsley James was loaned out to Blue Square Premier side Hereford United, managed by former Vale striker Martin Foyle.

Meanwhile, Calvin Andrew, who had initially joined on a short-term contract agreed a deal to remain until the end of the season.

"I believe he has the ability to play an important part in our squad between now and the end of the season."

– Micky Adams on Calvin Andrew, 28ᵗʰ January

However, the rest of the squad would have to wait until the summer to discuss their contracts as the club announced that contract talks were on hold until the Vale found out which division it was in. Judging by January's league position and the squad strengthening there was now a very good chance it could be League One.

League Two Table: end of January

	Club	GD	Points
1	Gillingham	+24	55
2	**Port Vale**	**+26**	**53**
3	Burton	+1	46
4	Northampton	+7	45
5	Exeter	+3	45

February: nerves start to jangle

"We aren't the finished article and we know that. What we have to do now is get back on track as soon as possible."

– Micky Adams, 17ᵗʰ February

On the 1st February, Port Vale announced that fans had voted "overwhelmingly" in favour to change the club crest for the 2013-14 campaign.

Meanwhile, manager Micky Adams was still keen to strengthen his squad. However, the manager did rule out signing former defender Lee Collins, who had been released by Barnsley.

"While we are happy with the numbers and the people we have available to us in our squad, once the loan window re-opens we might look again. But we are happy with what we have done."

– Micky Adams, 1st February

"Lee [Collins] has great affinity to this club. I thought he did fantastically well for me, but I can't see anything happening."

– Micky Adams, 1st February

Match Thirty Five
Opposition: At home to Accrington
Competition: League Two
Date: February 2, 2013
Scoreline: Port Vale 3-0 Accrington
Vale goals: Hughes (50, 66), Purse (54)
Attendance: 5,172

Pre-match quote: "We will pick a side accordingly and, as I said, the onus is on us to go and attack them. What we have got to do is move the ball early, set a high tempo in the game and take our chances when they come along." (Micky Adams)

Port Vale line-up: Neal, Duffy, Purse, Chilvers, Jones, Myrie-Williams (Andrew), Burge (Shuker), Loft, Vincent, Pope, Hughes (Williamson)

Match report snippet: "Port Vale returned to the top of the League Two table after a comprehensive home victory over ten-man Accrington at Vale Park." (OVF)

OVF man of the match: Ryan Burge

Post-match quote: "Our first-half performance was very disappointing. But we had a good talk at half-time to sort a few things out." (Micky Adams)

Match Thirty Six
Opposition: At home to Wimbledon
Competition: League Two
Date: February 5, 2013
Scoreline: Port Vale 3-0 Wimbledon
Vale goals: Hughes (13), Vincent (35, 75)
Attendance: 5,567

Pre-match quote: "At this time of the season it is about getting three points on the board." (Mark Grew)

Port Vale line-up: Neal, Duffy, Purse, Chilvers, Jones, Myrie-Williams (Birchall), Loft, Burge, Vincent (Andrew) Hughes (Williamson), Pope

Match report snippet: "Port Vale extended their lead at the top of League Two to four points by easing to victory over bottom-of-the-table AFC Wimbledon. Lee Hughes headed home his fourth goal in as many games from Ryan Burge's free-kick to give Vale the lead." (BBC)

OVF man of the match: Ryan Burge

Post-match quote: "We've created a nice gap and the other teams have a lot to do to catch us. I wouldn't say we are promotion favourites, but then again I'm not a bookie." (Micky Adams)

Vale were buzzing after two successive home victories and there was further good news for the fans as the club announced that striker Tom Pope had agreed a new two-year contract with the Valiants.

"I've made no secret of my desire to stay and I'm really pleased we have come to an agreement on a new deal."
– Tom Pope, 6th February

The Vale were delighted to have secured their top striker and Micky Adams appeared to change his mind on his players' contracts. Despite declaring in January that the players would have to wait to the summer to find out if they had a deal, Adams now indicated that contracts would be done before the end of the season.

"We've started with Tom, but there might be other players who will attract attention from other clubs. So over the next week or so, we'll discuss their future as well. So this time, I want to be talking to players before the end of the season, so I can have a bit of a break."

– Micky Adams, 8th February

Next up for the Valiants was a trip to relegation-threatened Barnet. After the two strong home victories, it was to prove a wake-up call for Micky Adams' side.

Match Thirty Seven
Opposition: Away to Barnet
Competition: League Two
Date: February 9, 2013
Scoreline: Barnet 0-0 Port Vale
Vale goals: none
Attendance: 2,398 (696 away)

Pre-match quote: "I used to watch him in the major tournaments when I was younger. He was one of the best central midfield players in the world and it will be great to play against him." (Ryan Burge on Barnet player-boss Edgar Davids)

Port Vale line-up: Neal, Duffy, Purse, Chilvers, Jones, Myrie-Williams, Loft, Burge (Shuker), Vincent (Andrew), Hughes (Morsy), Pope

Match report snippet: "Port Vale failed to make it nine points in seven days as they were held to a 0-0 draw by a battling and resilient Barnet side. Star performer Edgar Davids, serenaded with a chorus of "you're just a small Stevie Wonder" was applauded off the pitch by the Vale fans." (OVF)

OVF man of the match: Chris Neal

Post-match quote: "Barnet were fantastic, they were better than us. Edgar Davids ran the show at times." (Micky Adams)

Off the pitch, the Supporters Club held an AGM. The Supporters Club had played a vital role in keeping Vale afloat but the efforts had exhausted the committee members who announced that they would stand aside and allow fresh blood to take over. Ally Simcock was duly appointed the new Chair, replacing Pete Williams.

"We're handing over to a new committee with the supporters club in good health. We've helped steer the football club through rocky waters and now, with new owners, we can look forward to the future with optimism."
– Pete Williams, 13ᵗʰ February

However, there was some sad news as it was announced that former Vale chairman Bill Bell had passed away, aged 81. Bell had been Chairman during the successful John Rudge era and had been widely credited with modernising Vale Park.

"I have some big shoes to fill and hope to do him proud over the coming years."
– Chairman Paul Wildes tweets on Bill Bell, 12ᵗʰ February

Meanwhile, Micky Adams was preparing for a tough end to the season. The manager announced that no-one was leaving the club on loan as "anyone might be called upon at any time" while contract talks with captain Doug Loft had started.

Match Thirty Eight
Opposition: Home to Morecambe
Competition: League Two
Date: February 16, 2013
Scoreline: Port Vale 0-1 Morecambe
Vale goals: none
Attendance: 5,513

Pre-match quote: "We'll have to find ways of breaking them down but we must remain focused on defending and not switch off." (Micky Adams)

Port Vale line-up: Neal, Yates (Shuker), Duffy, Purse, Jones, Myrie-Williams, Loft, Burge, Vincent (Andrew), Pope, Hughes (Williamson)

Match report snippet: "Port Vale fell off top spot in League Two after defeat by 10-man Morecambe. The Shrimps broke the deadlock on 63 minutes when Gary McDonald's cross fell into the path of forward Lewis Alessandra who bundled the ball home." (BBC)

OVF man of the match: Dan Jones

Post-match quote: "We had a lack of imagination in the forward areas and we've got things to work on." (Micky Adams)

The week following the Morecambe game was dominated by BBC Radio Stoke's comprehensive interview with Chairman Paul Wildes in which the co-owner outlined his plans for the club.

Wildes' key proposals, 21st February:

- To re-lay the Vale Park pitch
- To complete the Lorne St stand with the new half being designated a 'family' stand
- Family season tickets and free admission to under-12s (the first club in the league to do so)
- A club superstore to be located on the Hamil Road side of the ground
- Online ticketing and an enhanced club shop website
- Kits would pay tribute to club history and heritage
- A 'long-term' training deal with the St George's Park complex in Burton
- Long-term plans for a 'Vale Lodge' to house a development squad and training facilities
- A ten year plan with the focus on encouraging families and youngsters and developing homegrown players through the development squad.

Match Thirty Nine
Opposition: Away to Torquay
Competition: League Two
Date: February 23, 2013
Scoreline: Torquay 0-1 Port Vale
Vale goals: Andrew (28)
Attendance: 2,679 (670 away)

Pre-match quote: "There is enough will and determination in our squad to bounce back." (Micky Adams)

Port Vale line-up: Neal, Duffy, McCombe, Purse, Jones, Myrie-Williams, Burge (Morsy), Loft, Vincent, Pope, Andrew

Match report snippet: "Port Vale secured their first away win since January 12th as they narrowly defeated Torquay United thanks to Calvin Andrew's first Vale goal." (OVF)

OVF man of the match: Darren Purse

Post-match quote: "We lost a game last week and we had a magnificent response today from a group of players who rolled their sleeves up and ground out a 1-0 win away from home. I can't ask any more of them. We have answered a few critics today." (Micky Adams)

There was some debate over who had scored the winning goal against Torquay. Doug Loft's shot looked to be going in until it was deflected by Calvin Andrew, but the big Vale forward was determined to claim his first goal for the club.

"I saw the ball coming straight towards me and I just tried to open my body up. It was definitely my goal."
– Calvin Andrew, 25th February

Ironically, Andrew could get a second chance upfront as an illness to Lee Hughes looked set to rule him out of Vale's game against Exeter.

On the 25th February, Vale announced a further short-term contract with the FA's St George's Park facility which would allow the squad to continue to use the centre's all-weather pitches. The deal was sorely needed as the bad weather was still preventing Vale from training properly.

"We welcome this opportunity to use St George's Park, which is arguably the best training facility in the country."
– Micky Adams, 25th Feburary

Match Forty
Opposition: At home to Exeter
Competition: League Two
Date: February 26, 2013
Scoreline: Port Vale 0-2 Exeter
Vale goals: none
Attendance: 4,480

Pre-match quote: "Wins are massive now, particularly with games coming thick and fast." (Darren Purse)

Port Vale line-up: Neal, Duffy, McCombe (Hughes), Purse, Jones, Myrie-Williams, Burge, Loft, Vincent (Taylor), Andrew (Dodds), Pope

Match report snippet: "Exeter were good value for a seventh win from their last nine away games as they secured a 2-0 victory at Port Vale. Dodds fired an effort against a post three minutes from time and that was the closest off-colour Vale came to a consolation goal." (Sporting Life)

OVF man of the match: Dan Jones

Post-match quote: "We've lost the last two home games and we'll have to find different avenues and ways to play here. We're as frustrated by it as the supporters are." (Micky Adams)

The home loss to Exeter had sparked some criticism of the team by fans. The side was going through a rough spell and the criticism reignited the debate about whether fans should remain positive at all times – or whether criticism by paying customers is warranted on occasion. Columnist Martin Tideswell was in no doubt:

"Fans have every right to criticise and question when things go wrong – just as they lavished praise on the team and the manager earlier in the season."

– Martin Tideswell, 1st March

The Exeter loss completed a topsy-turvy month for the Valiants. The Vale had started it in imperious home form with 3-0 wins over Accrington and Wimbledon but ended it with two home defeats with a good away win over Torquay sandwiched in between.

The next month would be crucial for Vale who needed to find their home form and stop the worrying blip becoming something more serious.

League Two Table: end of February

	Club	GD	Points
1	Gillingham	+25	65
2	**Port Vale**	**+30**	**63**
3	Burton	+10	59
4	Northampton	+10	58
5	Rotherham	+7	56

March: a serious 'blip'

"The things that we were doing right to get results we're not doing at the moment. This is a blip, no doubt about it."

- Micky Adams, 3rd March

"Promotion seems a million miles away at the moment."

- Micky Adams, 9th March

"What the players and the manager need right now is a cuddle."

- Norman Smurthwaite, 15th March

Match Forty One
Opposition: Away at Oxford
Competition: League Two
Date: March 2, 2013
Scoreline: Oxford 2-1 Port Vale
Vale goals: Loft (15)
Attendance: 6,322 (865 away)

Pre-match quote: "We have always said we have got a decent squad. It might be time for those who have been on the sidelines to have a run in the side, but we'll pick whatever we think is the best team to get a result." (Micky Adams)

Port Vale line-up: Neal, Duffy, Jones, McCombe, Purse, Myrie-Williams, Loft, Burge (Morsy), Andrew (Hughes), Williamson (Dodds), Pope

Match report snippet: "Captain Doug Loft's long-range effort was in vain as the Vale were defeated 2-1 by Oxford United at the Kassam Stadium... Vale once again dropped more points in their promotion push." (OVF)

OVF man of the match: Doug Loft

Post-match quote: "The things that we were doing right to get results we're not doing at the moment. There's no doubt we're lacking confidence. This is a blip, there's no doubt about it, but we'll get through it." (Micky Adams)

Vale fans in contrasting moods at Oxford [Photos: Pete Tindall]

Following the defeat to Oxford, Micky Adams suggested that he would look to make additions to his squad.

"There's no denying that some of our players aren't in form at the moment and we think bringing someone in who perhaps has that bit of confidence can help the team get back to where they were."

- Micky Adams, 4th March

Later that day, BBC Radio Stoke tweeted that a "fans' favourite" was set to return to the club. And following that comment, the club confirmed that the signing was former midfielder Anthony Griffith, who had joined the club on loan.

"He knows the club and he knows the majority of the players which will help him to settle in quickly and hit the ground running."

- Micky Adams on Anthony Griffith, 4th March

Griffith went straight into the squad for the fixture against Bradford. It was a crucial game and Adams made an appeal to the fans the day before the match.

"There's a lot of negativity around at the moment and that's not going to help anybody, so we need the supporters to be our 12ᵗʰ man."

- Micky Adams, 5ᵗʰ March

Match Forty Two
Opposition: At home to Bradford City
Competition: League Two
Date: March 5, 2013
Scoreline: Port Vale 0-0 Bradford
Vale goals: none
Attendance: 4,281

Pre-match quote: "We've got to be positive and look for three points. It's not a crisis, we just have players who are not at their best right now. (Mark Grew)

Port Vale line-up: Neal, Duffy, Chilvers, Purse, Jones, Myrie-Williams (Hughes), Loft, Griffith, Vincent (Morsy), Dodds, Pope

Match report snippet: "It was Vale's first goalless stalemate at home this season. For City, that made it back-to-back clean sheets." (Bradford Telegraph and Argus)

OVF man of the match: Louis Dodds

Post-match quote: "We have to take crumbs of comfort. It's a point on the board and a clean sheet against a good Bradford side." (Micky Adams)

The Bradford draw stretched Vale's winless run to three games as nerves started to jangle. Micky Adams again appealed to fans to remain calm and 'keep their nerve.'

"I've always said there would be twists and turns, but we've got to hold our nerve. There are ten games to go and thirty points to play for."

- Micky Adams, 8th March

"Sadly, I think Micky is a victim of his and the team's success this season. Before a ball was kicked I would have been very happy to have seen Vale in a safe mid-table position. However, our early success has raised the expectancy levels of fans. Anything short of automatic promotion will be seen as a failure by the majority of fans, which, is bizarre and unfair on the players and manager alike. Patience is needed by us fans."

- OVF blogger Malcolm Hirst, 8th March

There was some good news for Chris Birchall, whose return to the Vale had prompted Trinidad and Tobago to recall him for their latest round of International fixtures. Birchall, who made 22 International appearances during his first spell at the club, was the Vale's most-capped International player.

Match Forty Three
Opposition: At home to Southend
Competition: League Two
Date: March 9, 2013
Scoreline: Port Vale 1-2 Southend
Vale goals: Hughes (64)
Attendance: 4,858

Pre-match quote: "We have got some big games coming up against teams that are going to be in and around the promotion picture, as we can help ourselves. The good thing is we are in a good position and it is all about us and what we do." (Micky Adams)

Port Vale line-up: Neal, Duffy, Chilvers, Purse (McCombe), Taylor, Myrie-Williams (Birchall), Griffith, Morsy, Shuker (Andrew), Hughes, Pope

Match report snippet: "Lee Hughes scored his fifth Vale goal but Port Vale failed to win for the fourth game in a row." (OVF)

OVF man of the match: Sam Morsy

Post-match quote: "Promotion seems a million miles away at the moment. It was very disappointing and I'm fed up of saying the same things." (Micky Adams)

The Southend result only served to increase the tension at Vale Park and manager Micky Adams certainly seemed less confident about the team's chances of automatic promotion.

"The first target is to make sure we get enough points to get into the play-offs and then go from there."
- Micky Adams, 10th March

Adams also accepted personal responsibility for the team's poor form adding:

"We'll have to take a bit of stick and I will too. But I'm big enough to handle it and I want the players to be big enough as well."
- Micky Adams, 11th March

At least Adams was still receiving the full backing of the club's owners, despite the alarming recent form. Norman Smurthwaite took to Twitter to tell fans that "I pledge my support to MA [Micky Adams]."

Meanwhile, another regular Twitter user, Ryan Burge was fit enough to be included in the Vale squad for the trip to Bristol Rovers.

Match Forty Four
Opposition: Bristol Rovers
Competition: League Two
Date: March 12, 2013
Scoreline: Bristol Rovers 2-0 Port Vale
Vale goals: none
Attendance: 5,111 (203 away)

Pre-match quote: "We'll add Ryan Burge to that group [which faced Southend] and I'll pick a side to go and beat Bristol Rovers." (Micky Adams)

Port Vale line-up: Neal, Yates, Duffy (Vincent), Chilvers, McCombe, Taylor, Griffith, Birchall, Morsy, Williamson (Andrew), Pope (Hughes)

Match report snippet: "Ryan Brunt scored twice as Bristol Rovers beat Port Vale, who are now without a win in five matches." (BBC)

OVF man of the match: Sam Morsy

Post-match quote: "The real supporters need to get hold of the idiots and all of us pull in the right direction. Some of the stuff our supporters were coming out with tonight was disgusting." (Micky Adams)

It's fair to say that the aftermath of the Rovers' game was probably the most controversial episode of the entire season and it possibly came close to derailing the whole promotion bid.

The side's form was deteriorating rapidly and some fans were fulsome in their criticism of the club, despite the side still sitting in the promotion places.

Two things in particular caused upset and controversy – midfielder Ryan Burge's remarks on social media and Micky Adams' criticism of a section of the away support.

Following the final whistle, in an emotional post-match interview, Adams had lashed out at a section of the travelling fans for 'idiotic' abuse of players and himself.

Micky Adams' comments – the fallout

Some fans applauded Adams' willingness to challenge abuse and backed his call to fully support the club. Others felt it was disrespectful for the manager, who had said before the match that he expected and could take criticism, to label supporters who had traveled a great distance to support the team (and who should be allowed to express their views) as 'idiots'.

The fans in the best position to judge the outburst were those present on the night. Many of the away fans didn't think Adams was simply responding badly to the 'regular' abuse and criticism that a poor away defeat brings. The view of many of those present was that the personal abuse of Adams and in particular his family by a tiny minority *was so* abusive and so beyond the pale that it was understandable why the manager had snapped.

Paul Wildes tried to calm the matter down. He told the *Sentinel*: "It doesn't help players' confidence if supporters get on their backs, but we know they're only doing it because they're desperate to see the team win." CEO Norman Smurthwaite added that the players and manager simply needed a "cuddle."

After the furore caused by the comments, it was noticeable that many subsequent club statements were much more complimentary towards the "tremendous" fans. Perhaps the dispute had shown the club that criticism of the supporters, regardless of whether it was justified or not, had the potential to lose a portion of the support? If so, it had learnt a valuable lesson.

If the reaction to Micky Adams' comments was mixed, then the response to social media remarks by Ryan Burge eventually proved to be much more clear-cut.

Burge's tweets

Ryan Burge @RyanJBurge   39 mins
5 mins from Bristol and told not to bother coming, I'm not needed for the game. #cheers

Ryan Burge @RyanJBurge   11 hrs
If u believe anything else u may aswell believe I was ill or late saturday. This is all I will say.
Expand

Ryan Burge @RyanJBurge   11 hrs
After numerous unanswered calls and txts the one time I hear anything back it's a message to tell me to go home I'm not needed
Expand

Ryan Burge @RyanJBurge   11 hrs
For starters the plan was for me to be picked up by the coach at Michael wood services, I should never have been making my own way there
Expand

Initially, fans' sympathies were with Burge, who had impressed in midfield and whose presence in midfield may have prevented the disappointing loss to Rovers.

But as more facts emerged and the club responded, the club's decision not to play the midfielder was generally accepted. The key fact in the dispute was the remark by Micky Adams that Burge had not turned up for a 4:30pm team meeting. As Burge's tweet was sent at 6:30pm, he was already two hours late by that point.

Many fans saw Burge's behaviour as unacceptable and felt that Adams had no choice but to drop him from the squad. Ironically, the fans' backing of the club's response helped to repair some of the disenchantment caused by Adams' earlier remarks.

Burge's tweet – the reaction

"He should have been at the hotel at 4.30pm and he still wasn't there at 5.15, so what am I supposed to do? Then he puts a load of rubbish on his Twitter feed. It's absolute nonsense and he's going to be disciplined." (Micky Adams)

"Ryan has been silly and we will deal with it internally. We have to remember he's a young lad. He's got it wrong on this occasion, but that doesn't mean he has no future at the club. That will be for Micky to decide." (Paul Wildes)

After all the drama, it was crucial that the fan base didn't split as it had done under the previous reviled regimes. OVF launched an appeal called "Bin the boos… back the boys" with Rob Fielding commenting "Now it is surely the time to put personal differences aside, to back every player in a Vale shirt."

In an interview, far removed from his angry Bristol Rovers post-match comments, Micky Adams also seemed keen to rebuild bridges with the fans.

"We appreciate the support, so get behind the lads and let's try and get ourselves out of this mess."
- Micky Adams, 15th March

Meanwhile, the club's stance over Burge seemed to have softened. The midfielder was included in the squad to travel to York, the club's next match and on March the 15th the midfielder issued a partial apology via Twitter.

Burge's tweets – the 'apology'

Ryan Burge @RyanJBurge   10m
Was very angry and frustrated the other night, however...
Expand

Ryan Burge @RyanJBurge   9m
in future won't be using twitter to show that will be using alternative
options that won't cause any upset or anxiety to the fans/club
Expand

However, Burge's second tweet seemed somewhat ambiguous. Was the midfielder accepting he should not criticise the club *per se* or was he suggesting that he would now use "alternative options" to put forward his version of events?

The club's reaction to the tweets was swift. Hours after they had appeared, the decision to include Burge in the squad was reversed and a club statement announced that the midfielder had been suspended for 14 days.

"We asked Ryan to apologise for his statements on Twitter on Thursday and Ryan declined to do this. Although we note that Ryan has now issued something on his twitter feed, this has come too late."

- Paul Wildes in a club statement, 15th March

TWITTER GUIDELINES

Players should not tweet three hours before a game and until post-match responsibilities are fulfilled.

Posts must be in good taste and not contain vulgar or obscene words or images.

Tweets should not broadcast private or time-sensitive information about the organisation, including team selection.

Tweets should not openly criticise team or Club officials, including other members of the playing squad. This extends to referees and other match officials.

BY ORDER OF THE MANAGER

OVF sponsored the home game against Aldershot Town and the pre-match tour of the dressing room enabled this photo of the club's Twitter guidelines to be taken. [Photo: onevalefan.co.uk]

Match Forty Five
Opposition: Away at York
Competition: League Two
Date: 16 March, 2013
Scoreline: York City 0-2 Port Vale
Vale goals: Myrie-Williams (7), Hughes (48)
Attendance: 3,945 (1,035 away)

Pre-match quote: "We're going through one of those periods of form that hit many teams. But we have enough character in the dressing room to get ourselves out of the mess we're in." (Micky Adams)

Port Vale line-up: Neal, Yates, McCombe, Chilvers, Taylor, Myrie-Williams (Andrew) , Griffith, Dodds (Shuker), Hughes (Williamson), Pope

Match report snippet: "Phew! Micky Adams' side earned their first win in six games after goals from Jennison Myrie-Williams and Lee Hughes secured a vital 2-0 away win over York." (OVF)

OVF man of the match: Jennison Myrie-Williams

Post-match quote: "I feel a lot of relief I think and I'm pleased for the people that matter - the supporters." (Micky Adams)

In the aftermath of the Bristol Rovers fans criticism, the club was once again swift to praise supporters for their backing following the crucial win over York.

Louis Dodds commented that the "fans have been fantastic all season" while Adam Yates added that "the supporters were fantastic at York."

Striker Tom Pope was unsurprisingly named on the shortlist for the prestigious League Two player of the season, but there was a blow for Chris Birchall as OVF revealed that due to time differences and travelling time while on International duty, the midfielder was now likely to miss the next two Vale games.

The club also announced that it would be paying tribute to 1994, the year the club was last promoted, during the game against Burton. Prices were slashed to '94 levels and members of Vale's previous promotion team would be paraded on the pitch.

Vale fans naturally hoped that by the time the Burton game arrived that they too would be celebrating promotion and not looking nervously over their shoulders at the chasing pack.

Meanwhile, Mark Grew was being pragmatic and told the Sentinel that the side may have to win ugly to get over the finishing line.

"We're looking at the possibility of playing more direct. We're not going to totally change the system, but we might decide to play a more percentage game."
– Mark Grew, 19th March

However, the side would not have a chance to demonstrate their direct style as the club's next game – at home to Aldershot fell victim of the bad weather. Nevertheless, there were still copious Vale celebrations during the weekend as Tom Pope was crowned League Two player of the year and Jennison Myrie-Williams was named as one of the top ten players in the division.

"I'm just a local lad who has tried his best and had a good season. Individual records and accolades are great, but it will mean nothing unless we win promotion."

- League Two player of the year Tom Pope, 26th March

However, Mark Grew soon put a dampener on the celebrations with a reminder of the huge Easter fixtures against Cheltenham and Chesterfield.

"In the context of the season, these fixtures are massive. It's a double whammy and they could play a big part in how things pan out."

- Mark Grew, 26th March

Match Forty Six
Opposition: At home to Cheltenham
Competition: League Two
Date: 29 March, 2013
Scoreline: Port Vale 3-2 Cheltenham
Vale goals: Pope (19, 58, 74)
Attendance: 5,867

Pre-match quote: "They are a big strong side and I think that anybody who went to Cheltenham earlier on in the season to watch the game will have seen what they are about." (Tom Pope)

Port Vale line-up: Neal, Yates, McCombe, Chilvers, Jones, Myrie-Williams, Griffith, Dodds, Taylor (Andrew), Hughes (Williamson), Pope

Match report snippet: "Tom Pope ended his barren spell as he fired a hat-trick to earn Port Vale a dramatic 3-2 victory over Cheltenham on Good Friday. With league leaders Gillingham not in action, Micky Adams' side had a chance to move to within five points of the npower League Two leaders." (Daily Mail)

OVF man of the match: Tom Pope

Post-match quote: "Tom was superb. He was the catalyst to what we did. He's a local boy who is desperate to do well for the club he has supported since he was a boy. He epitomises the spirit we've got here. Some people have questioned that spirit and we have had a difficult spell, but we are a close-knit group and days like this bring us even closer." (Micky Adams)

After the match, 'Micky Adams praised Pope's Easter service' (as the OVF headline proclaimed) after Vale ended a difficult month with two very welcome results and remained on course for an automatic promotion place.

"When there was a forward pass on we played it forward, when there was a cross on we put the ball into the box. We told them not to take the easy option because a positive mindset is vital when the going gets tough."

- Micky Adams, 30th March

League Two table: end of March

	Club	GD	Points
1	Gillingham	+27	76
2	**Port Vale**	**+29**	**70**
3	Northampton	+11	68
4	Burton	+9	66
5	Cheltenham	+6	66

April: finishing the job

"We've got to stand up and be counted."
– Mark Grew, 18th April

"If Burton was huge then this is colossal."
– Martin Tideswell, 18th April

"We're Vale. We're united. By 5pm on Saturday, let's hope we're in League One."
 – Rob Fielding, 18th April

Match Forty Seven
Opposition: Away to Chesterfield
Competition: League Two
Date: 1 April, 2013
Scoreline: Chesterfield 2-2 Port Vale
Vale goals: Purse (5), Pope (85)
Attendance: 6,669 (2,040 away)

Pre-match quote: "Every game between now and the end of the season is going to be difficult and if we are not going to be up for it and put the effort in then we are going to get beat." (Tom Pope)

Port Vale line-up: Neal, Yates, Purse, Chilvers, Jones, Myrie-Williams, Loft, Griffith (Williamson), Taylor (Birchall), Andrew (Shuker), Pope

Match report snippet: "Tom Pope came up with an important sting in the tail as Port Vale earned what could turn out to be a crucial draw. And make no mistake, Port Vale will look back at yesterday's result as a point gained, rather than two lost." (Sentinel)

OVF man of the match: Adam Yates/Doug Loft

Post-match quote: "We won't know until the end of the season how important this result is but looking at the other results, it's a massive point for us." (Micky Adams)

The draw at Chesterfield had given Vale a welcome boost and interest in the Burton game was now high. Vale were reporting impressive ticket sales as fans took advantage of the reduced 1994 era prices.

The Burton game was being seen as a crucial moment in Vale's season. The visitors were pushing to catch Vale in what looked to be a classic promotion six pointer.

"No doubt about it, it is a big game. If we get a positive result it can put six-seven points between us. They are not going to come here to draw... it should be an entertaining game."

- Chris Neal, 4th April

And as match day neared, the Valiants (once again using Twitter to good effect) kept reporting better and better ticket sales. A few hours before kick-off the club reported that both the Lorne St stand and the Railway Paddock had sold-out for arguably the most important game of the season...

Match Forty Eight
Opposition: Home to Burton
Competition: League Two
Date: 5 April, 2013
Scoreline: Port Vale 7-1 Burton
Vale goals: Hughes (12, 22, 51 pen), Birchall (25), Pope (56), Williamson (73, 90)
Attendance: 10,978

Pre-match quote: "It's a big game for us, but we can't go out looking to win the game in the first five minutes. It's a 90-minute game and if we win it in the 89th, then I'll be happy." (Doug Loft)

Port Vale line-up: Neal, Yates, Purse, Chilvers, Jones, Myrie-Williams (Dodds), Griffith (Shuker), Birchall, Loft, Hughes (Williamson), Pope

Match report snippet: "Vale's biggest crowd for 15 years saw Vale take a giant step towards automatic promotion with an astonishing 7-1 home win over Burton." (OVF)

OVF man of the match: Lee Hughes

Post-match quote: "We want more of this, so let's hope we have another special night on Tuesday." (Micky Adams)

The crushing win over Burton, in front of Vale Park's biggest crowd for 15 years gave the whole club a huge boost as it looked to seal the all-important promotion.

It had been an emotional evening with John Rudge and members of the 1994 promotion and Autoglass Trophy winning sides being cheered onto the pitch at half-time. The three points were vital but it had also given owners Wildes and Smurthwaite a glimpse of the club's potential.

As several fans remarked afterwards, following all the trials and tribulations of recent years; the battles against the board, the protests, the months in administration; just who would have though the Vale would be cheered off the pitch by a packed Vale Park crowd after thrashing their promotion rivals?

"The performance was fuelled by the supporters. I saw the potential here, the supporters showed that and I thank each one of them. It was nice that the team from 1994 were there to see it. We wanted to put on a show."

- Micky Adams, 6th April

A packed Railway stand at the Burton game [Photo: Jordan Phillips]

Match Forty Nine
Opposition: Home to Aldershot
Competition: League Two
Date: 9 April, 2013
Scoreline: Port Vale 1-1 Aldershot
Vale goals: Myrie-Williams (45)
Attendance: 6,197

Pre-match quote: "Tomorrow is an absolutely vital game for us. If we can get another win, then we're nearly there." (Chris Birchall)

Port Vale line-up: Neal, Yates, Purse, McCombe (Davis), Jones, Myrie-Williams, Griffith, Birchall (Andrew), Loft, Hughes (Williamson), Pope

Match report snippet: "While a frustrating 1-1 draw fell short of fans' expectations against a team at the bottom of the table, the point gained takes Vale one step closer to their ultimate goal." (Sentinel)

OVF man of the match: Anthony Griffith

Post-match quote: "It certainly didn't go as we planned but credit to Aldershot, they deserved their point and could have taken all three. If that's the case, then we're lucky people." (Micky Adams)

The Aldershot draw wasn't the result that everyone wanted but nevertheless Vale still kept their place in the automatic promotion spots.

On the 12th April, to no great surprise, it was announced that midfielder Ryan Burge had left by 'mutual consent.' It was a sad end to Burge's Vale career.

"This has been a difficult decision for both parties and we would like to wish Ryan the very best success in the next step of his career."
- Paul Wildes, 12th April

Despite the Burge departure, the supporter-base was still buzzing after the Burton win and Paul Wildes continued the feel-good factor by announcing that the club's owners would continue to invest to take Vale higher up the leagues.

Ryan Burge pictured in pre-season friendly action
[Photo: onevalefan.co.uk]

In an interview with the *BBC 'Late Kick-Off'* programme, Wildes commented that "We've invested a lot of time and effort in making the club better... things that a normal commercial business should have - the fans are our customers and we have to improve the service we offer them."

But all the off-field activities were very much secondary to events on the pitch. After recovering from their sticky patch and with three games remaining, the Valiants were now potentially a win away from sealing promotion, providing results elsewhere went their way.

The first of those three crucial games was an away trip to Rochdale.

Match Fifty
Opposition: Away to Rochdale
Competition: League Two
Date: 13 April, 2013
Scoreline: Rochdale 2-2 Port Vale
Vale goals: Pope (34), Chilvers (89)
Attendance: 5042 (2,900 away *)

* approximate figure, away crowd not confirmed

Pre-match quote: "My assistant manager went to watch them on Wednesday night and they were very, very good. He came back in a really positive frame of mind about them and that is worrying." (Micky Adams)

Port Vale line-up: Neal, Yates, Purse, Chilvers, Jones, Griffith, Loft, Dodds (Morsy), Myrie-Williams (Duffy), Pope, Hughes (McCombe)

Match report snippet: "For a fleeting moment, it looked as though Vale were on their way to League One. Liam Chilvers had made up for his earlier own goal by thumping in an 89th-minute header and nearly 3,000 travelling fans were ready to start the promotion party. But less than five minutes later, the mood had changed dramatically as Rochdale grabbed an even later equaliser." (Sentinel)

OVF man of the match: Adam Yates

Post-match quote: "It was an emotional rollercoaster..." (Micky Adams)

It was an agonising result, Vale had appeared to clinch promotion through Chilvers' goal, only for a late goal and results elsewhere to halt the celebrations. Vale would still need points against Northampton and Wycombe to be mathematically sure of promotion.

The club looked to do everything possible to make the side's task easier – with the main focus on packing Vale Park to provide as much support for the Valiants as possible.

Announcing a special deal for Northampton on Monday morning we want to set the highest attendance in Lg 2 #recordbreakers #packthepark
- a tweet from Paul Wildes, 13th April

That 'deal' turned out to be the chance to refund the cost of the match ticket against next season's season ticket – but without the reduced ticket prices that Vale had offered against Burton was there really any chance of a five figure crowd?

Well, the signs were that supporters were turning up in force to lend their support. Vale fans from Australia, Scandinavia and the USA were on the way to Burslem.

Tickets were selling at a phenomenal rate and the club soon announced that the Railway Stand, Paddock and Lorne Street stand had all completely sold-out.

"It will be a united crowd – united in its support of Micky Adams and the players, united in its support of the owners, their professionalism and vision for the future – and united in hoping that the club can finally seal one of the most extraordinary seasons in Port Vale's history with promotion. We're Vale. We're united. By 5pm on Saturday, let's hope... we're in League One."

- Rob Fielding, 19th April.

Now it was time for the match itself. The Valiants simply needed to avoid defeat and providing results elsewhere went their way, the club would be promoted.

Match Fifty One
Opposition: Home to Northampton
Competition: League Two
Date: 20 April, 2013
Scoreline: Port Vale 2-2 Northampton
Vale goals: Chilvers (38), Collins (86 own-goal)
Attendance: 12,496

Pre-match quote: "We all know the enormity of this game. We all know what's at stake. The players have seen the queues for tickets and they know what it means. We have a fantastic chance to create a bit of history, and I want to make sure we do." (Micky Adams)

Port Vale line-up: Neal, Yates, Purse (Shuker), Chilvers, Jones, Myrie-Williams, Griffith (Morsy), Dodds (Birchall), Loft, Hughes, Pope

Match report snippet: "Former Valiant Lee Collins provided a crucial own-goal as the Vale came from behind to secure a point and all but secure promotion to League One." (OVF)

OVF man of the match: Liam Chilvers

Post-match quote: "What the players have achieved has been a minor miracle in the circumstances and I couldn't be more proud of them." (Micky Adams)

The final whistle at the end of the Northampton game was greeted by delight by Vale fans. Only a 28 goal reverse in the final fixture could prevent the Valiants rising into League One. Jubilant fans invaded the pitch overjoyed with the side's achievement while players and their families celebrated on the turf.

Fans on the pitch after the final whistle [Photo: Alex Woolgar]

Tom Pope is carried aloft by supporters [Photo: Rob Machin]

Tickertape covers the fans [Photo: onevalefan.co.uk]

A congregation of "Popes" [Photo: Barry Bevington]

Darren Purse celebrates with his family [Photo: Robert Morris]

"I've been blubbering after the game, but now I've settled down I'm absolutely delighted for everyone connected with the football club."

- Micky Adams, 20th April

"The fans have been terrific. Us going up is for them."

- Captain Doug Loft, 20th April

"You couldn't have scripted it any differently."

Adam Yates, 20th April

"It hasn't sunk in yet but after about twenty pints tonight, I will reflect on it."

- Striker Tom Pope, 20th April

The result had given the owners food for thought and Chairman Paul Wildes was not slow in claiming that the side could build on the promotion.

"We want this club to keep going forward, and I'd say we're as big a club as many in League One, so why not? Promotion is a big step and one we needed to take, but now we'll look for the next one to take this club back to where it belongs. We don't want to get ahead of ourselves, but we have no debts so let's go for it."

- Paul Wildes, 22nd April

Now, with promotion all but mathematically assured, there was just the final game against Wycombe to come. To add a little spice to the occasion, former Valiant Gareth Ainsworth, now player-manager at Wycombe, announced that the game would be his final match as a player. With Vale potentially not even needing a point to cement promotion, the stage was set for a double celebration...

Match Fifty Two
Opposition: Away to Wycombe
Competition: League Two
Date: 27 April, 2013
Scoreline: Wycombe 1-1 Port Vale
Vale goals: Hughes (79)
Attendance: 7120 (2,828 away)

Pre-match quote: "The club's always bigger than me but I might try and have my little moment on Saturday. I don't think anyone will begrudge me that." (Gareth Ainsworth)

Port Vale line-up: Neal, Duffy (Myrie-Williams), Purse, McCombe, Jones, Loft, Morsy (Lloyd), Birchall, Shuker, Vincent (Hughes), Pope

Match report snippet: "The Valiants mathematically sealed promotion after a 1-1 draw at Wycombe in a game which marked the end of Vale legend Gareth Ainsworth's final game as a player." (OVF)

OVF man of the match: Doug Loft

Post-match quote: "I'm pleased it's over, I'm delighted for everyone connected with the football club that we've had a fantastic season. I can't pay the players high enough praise they've been absolutely terrific." (Micky Adams)

Celebrations at the Wycombe game
[Photos: Pete Tindall and Steve Mellor]

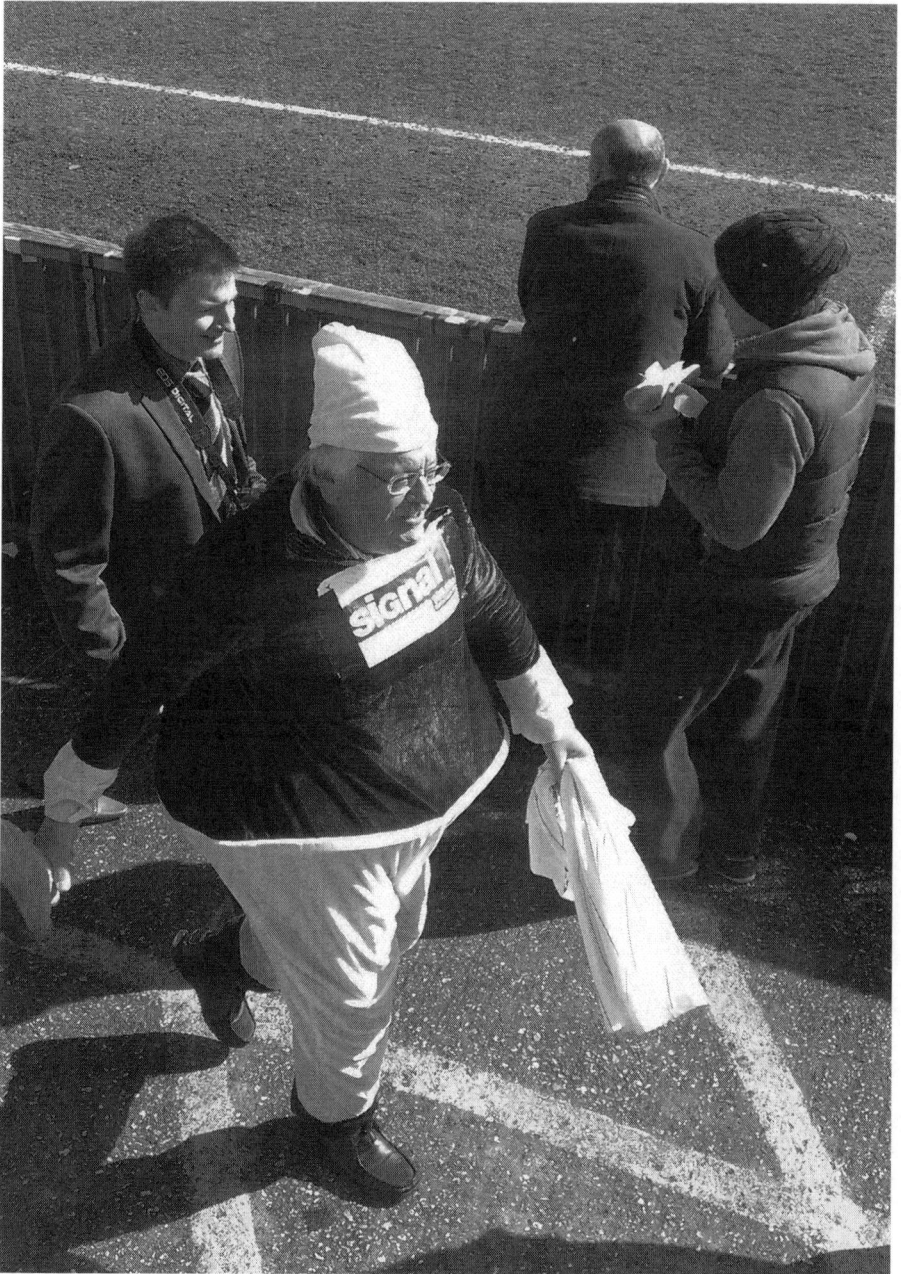

Few clubs can boast a CEO as charismatic as Norman Smurthwaite,
seen here wearing a "Smurf" fancy-dress outfit at Wycombe
[Photo: Steve Mellor]

Feeding the Popes and fans before the game [Photos: Ray Aldi]

"This achievement will surely rank among English football's greatest comebacks – a tribute to Port Vale's fans, its players, the coaching staff and the club's new owners."
- Martin Tideswell

"It's a minor miracle."

- Micky Adams

Micky Adams: Had worked a 'minor miracle' [Photo: Robert Morris]

The draw against Wycombe had allowed rivals Rotherham to sneak in and secure second place, but frankly no-one in Burslem cared a jot. Promotion was confirmed and Vale had a "p" next to their name. They were going to play in League One next season.

Arguably, this campaign was the most thrilling in the club's entire 137 year history. The Vale had experienced plenty of highs and far too many lows but no other season came close to the sheer drama of 2012-2013.

A campaign that began with the collapse of the Keith Ryder deal, player contractual issues, the lack of a kit deal and the club in administration had been transformed. A takeover, the team's form and the erection of a statue to a club legend had helped to unite the fans after years of unrest.

Vale had ended the year on top of the table but that momentum had almost stalled after controversy in Bristol and a New Year slump. But despite all the distractions, both on and off the field, manager Micky Adams had worked wonders and achieved something that no fan would have predicted at the start of the campaign.

From despair to delight, from administration to promotion, it had been no ordinary season.

[Photo: Anthony Cheatham]

League Two Table: end of April

	Club	GD	Points
1	Gillingham (C)	+27	83
2	Rotherham (P)	+15	79
3	**Port Vale (P)**	**+35**	**78**
4	Burton	+6	76
5	Cheltenham	+7	75

OVF player of the season

The onevalefan.co.uk website (OVF) ran a poll asking fans for their man of the match for every first-team game of the 2012-13 season. Here is the final leaderboard:

6 votes:
Chris Neal, Ryan Burge, Tom Pope
5 votes:
Sam Morsy, Louis Dodds, Doug Loft
4 votes:
Jennison Myrie-Williams
3 votes:
Dan Jones, Adam Yates
2 votes:
Darren Purse, Clayton McDonald,
1 vote:
Sam Johnson, Ben Williamson, John McCombe, Lee Hughes, Liam Chilvers, Anthony Griffith

National awards

- nPower League Managers' Association Performance of the week: Port Vale 6-2 Rotherham, September 8th
- nPower League Two manager of the month for September: Micky Adams
- nPower League Two player of the month for September: Tom Pope
- nPower League Two player of the month for October: Ashley Vincent
- nPower League Two player of the year: Tom Pope
- Match of the Day magazine League Two player of the year: Tom Pope
- Players named in Football League Two top ten players of the season: Tom Pope (1st), Jennison Myrie-Williams (5th)

Player of the Year awards

- Player of the year: Tom Pope
- Young player of the year: Sam Johnson
- Youth team player of the year: Doug Price
- Away player of the year: Chris Neal
- Players' player of the year: Chris Neal
- Goal of the season: Louis Dodds (versus Fleetwood)

Pope's records

- Tom Pope became the first Vale player to score three hat-tricks at Vale Park in one season.

- On the 6th October, Pope became the fastest Vale player to reach double figures since Tom Nolan in 1933. Pope scored twice at Exeter to take his tally to 11 goals in 13 games.

- The striker became the fastest Vale player to score 20 goals in the season beating Wilf Kirkham's record. Pope reached the tally of 20 goals in 23 games with a hat-trick against Bristol Rovers.

- Pope also became the first Stoke-on-Trent-born player to score 20-plus goals in a season since Robbie Earle in the 1988-1989 season.

- He finished as the season's top scorer in all four divisions of the Football and Premier League with 33 goals to his name.

Trivia

- Tom Pope had given fans a glimpse of his newfound goal-scoring prowess in the pre-season friendlies. Pope had scored eleven goals in nine appearances including eight goals in two games (four goals in the 5-0 thrashing of Irish side Athlone Town and a further four in the 9-0 win over Shiven Rangers).

- Pope was 80-1 at the start of the season to finish as the League Two highest scorer

- At the start of the season Vale were ranked 18 out of 24 clubs to get promotion by the bookies

- Four players started their second spell with the Valiants during the season. They were Jennison Myrie-Williams (previously on loan in 2011), Liam Chilvers (also previously on loan in 2011), Chris Birchall (first spell 2001 to 2006) and Anthony Griffith (previous spell 2008-2012)

- Vale's home attendance against Burton in April (10,978) was the club's highest attendance for 15 years.

- Seventeen different players scored for the club during the season.

- Port Vale's mammoth penalty shoot-out against Walsall in the Johnstone's Paints Trophy lasted for twenty two attempts with both goalkeepers taking kicks.

- In all campaigns, Vale scored 96 goals

Player stats

NAME	2012-2013		VALE CAREER	
	GAMES	GOALS	GAMES	GOALS
Andrew	8+16	1	8+16	1
Birchall	5+6	1	63+39	9
Burge	26+8	3	28+9	3
Chilvers	20+1	2	32+1	2
Davis	5+5	0	11+7	0
Dodds	28+8	7	148+64	40
Duffy	38+1	1	38+1	1
Griffith	10	0	182+9	2
Hughes	13+5	10	13+5	10
James	4+3	0	4+8	0
Johnson	1	0	1	0
Jones	16	1	16	1
Lloyd	0+7	0	0+10	0
Loft	35+1	1	134+19	10
McAllister	1+2	0	1+2	0
McCombe	36+1	1	206+5	16
McDonald	23+3	1	48+11	1
Morsy	25+7	2	49+29	4
Murphy	1+2	0	1+2	0
Myrie-Williams	49+1	11	55+1	12
Neal	51	0	51	0
Owen	1+1	0	124+5	2
Pope	51	33	98+11	41
Purse	17	2	17	2
Shuker	17+17	1	29+21	2
Taylor	17+15	0	115+58	19
Vincent	38+2	8	38+2	8
Williamson	11+28	9	22+53	12
Yates	25+7	0	146+19	2

Player profiles

Goalkeepers

CHRIS NEAL: Signed on a free transfer, the keeper was hailed as one of the signings of the season. Reliable and unflappable, he was ever-present in the league.

Appearances: 51

SAM JOHNSON: A graduate of the Vale youth system, Johnson made a headline-grabbing debut in a Johnstone's Paints Trophy tie against Walsall. The six foot six inches tall keeper made three saves in the penalty shoot-out and scored the winning goal himself.

Appearances: 1

Defenders

RICHARD DUFFY: The experienced former Wales International joined on a free transfer in the summer. He proved his versatility with occasional spells at centre-back but for most of the campaign he battled Adam Yates for the right-back spot.
Appearances: 37+1 **Goals:** 0

ADAM YATES: The locally-born defender's place looked in jeopardy following the signing of Richard Duffy, but he knuckled down and was back as regular first-choice right-back by the end of the season.
Appearances: 25+7 **Goals:** 0

JOE DAVIS: The young graduate of the youth team was used sparingly after an error in the club's first game against Burnley.
Appearances: 5+5 **Goals:** 0

CLAYTON MCDONALD: The towering defender was a regular in the first-half of the season but found himself out of favour after Christmas and he ended the season on loan to Bristol Rovers.
Appearances: 23+3 **Goals:** 1

Clayton McDonald: a fine first-half of the season but fell out of favour afterwards [Photo: Robert Morris]

JOHN MCCOMBE: The tall defender was a regular starter throughout the season. Perhaps the only disappointing aspects of his season were a red card against Northampton and for someone who is normally a threat from set-pieces, just the solitary goal for the season.

Appearances: 36+1 **Goals:** 1

GARETH OWEN: The veteran had a low-key end to his Valiants' career as injuries took their toll. He was released in January and opted to retire from the game.

Appearances: 1+1 **Goals:** 0

LIAM CHILVERS: The experienced centre-half joined Vale for a second spell in November. A cool head at the back, Chilvers' previously unheralded goal ability came to the fore in the final stages with goals against Rochdale and Northampton.

Appearances: 20+1 **Goals:** 2

DARREN PURSE: The powerful veteran joined on a free transfer in the January transfer window and immediate made his presence felt in the Vale backline. His age meant he wasn't able to play every game in the run-in but during those he did play, he certainly gave his all.

Appearances: 17 **Goals:** 2

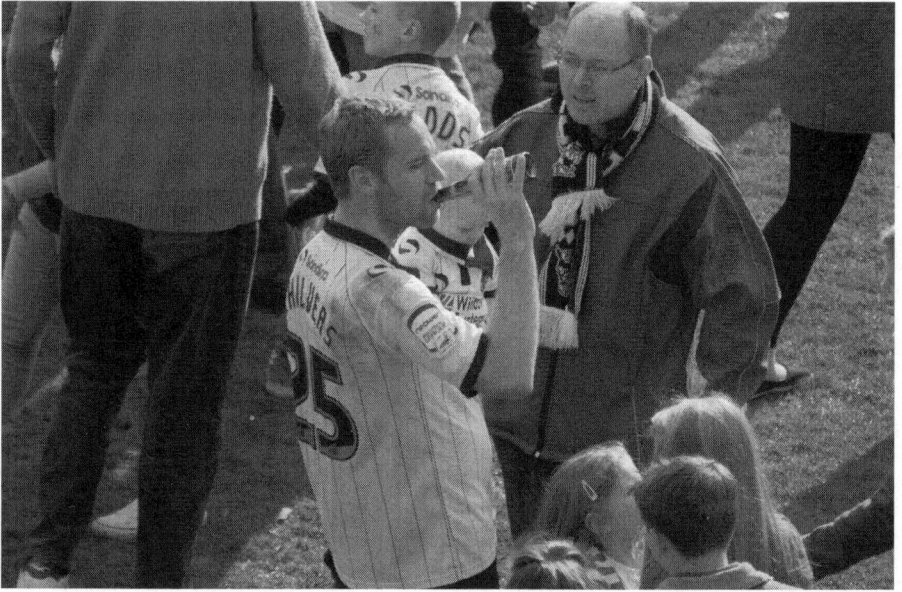

Liam Chilvers celebrates at the end of the Northampton game
[Photo: Robert Morris]

DAN JONES: A tall, pacy left-back, Jones was signed on a free transfer following his release by Sheffield Wednesday. He made an immediate impact with a goal on his debut during the televised game with AFC Wimbledon.

Appearances: 16 **Goals:** 1

Midfielders

SAM MORSY: Another graduate from the youth ranks, Morsy enjoyed a good start to the season but he blotted his copybook with a sending-off against Rochdale. He started fewer games after that incident but remained a valuable squad member for the remainder of the season.

Appearances: 25+7 **Goals:** 2

RYAN BURGE: After an injury-ravaged first season with the club, Burge bounced back to become a regular in the Vale midfield. But a late appearance for a team meeting followed by a controversial tweet before the game against Bristol Rovers and the lack of an apology for his actions saw him leave the club in April 2013.

Appearances: 26+9 **Goals:** 3

KINGSLEY JAMES: The young midfielder broke through to the first-team for a spell in December with the highlight being an appearance against former club Sheffeld United in the FA Cup. He was used more sparingly in 2013 and finished the season on loan to Hereford United.

Appearances: 4+3 **Goals:** 0

DOUG LOFT: The Vale club captain enjoyed another good season albeit one interrupted by injury on occasion. Showing his versatility, Loft played in a number of positions including left-back, left-midfield as well as his favoured central midfield role.

Appearances: 35+1 **Goals:** 1

CHRIS SHUKER: The diminutive midfielder started the season as first-choice in midfield and even after losing his starting place, he remained a valuable member of the Vale squad.

Appearances: 17+17 **Goals:** 1

DARREN MURPHY: The luckless Irishman had an injury-ravaged spell with the club and was released in January after a Vale career totaling just 75 minutes.

Appearances: 1+2 **Goals:** 0

Captain Doug Loft made 36 appearances
[Photo: onevalefan.co.uk]

CHRIS BIRCHALL: The Trinidad and Tobago International rejoined the club in January after a spell in US football. He scored against Burton in Vale's 7-1 win and also played twice for his country thus further extending his record as Vale's most-capped International player.

Appearances: 5+6 **Goals:** 1

SEAN MCALLISTER: A short-term signing, former Shrewsbury midfielder McAllister failed to make much of an impact, appearing just three times before being released in January.

Appearances: 1+2 **Goals:** 0

ANTHONY GRIFFITH: Yet another player to return for a second spell with the club, Griffith added his ball-winning skills to the midfield for the crucial run-in to the season.

Appearances: 10 **Goals:** 0

RYAN LLOYD: The young winger, another graduate from the youth ranks, was used only sporadically during the campaign.

Appearances: 0+7 **Goals:** 0

Anthony Griffith: enjoyed his second spell with the club after a loan move from Orient [Photo: onevalefan.co.uk]

JENNISON MYRIE-WILLIAMS: Another successful summer signing, winger Myrie-Williams enjoyed a good season, scoring eleven goals and providing umpteen chances for top-scorer Tom Pope.
Appearances: 49+1 **Goals:** 11

ASHLEY VINCENT: Vincent had a season of two halves, enjoying a flying start to the campaign but suffering in the second-half due to a combination of loss of form and injury.
Appearances: 38+2 **Goals:** 8

ROB TAYLOR: Another valuable squad player, Taylor did a decent job filling in at left-back or left-winger when required.
Appearances: 17+15 **Goals:** 0

Forwards

TOM POPE: The locally-born striker enjoyed one of the most memorable seasons in recent memory. He became the quickest Vale player to score twenty goals in a season, the first Vale player to score three hat-tricks in a season at Vale Park and capped a fine individual season with the League Two player of the year award.
Appearances: 51 **Goals:** 33

LEE HUGHES: After a failed attempt to sign the veteran on loan in November, the club finally signed Hughes in the January transfer window. He showed his quality with a goal on his debut and weighed in with a valuable ten goals in the crucial run-in period including a hat-trick against Burton Albion.
Appearances: 13+5 **Goals:** 10

LOUIS DODDS: One of the best natural finishers in the squad, Dodds had another decent season as a Vale player. He only scored seven goals but his link-up play with top-scorer Tom Pope was widely praised as was his ability to play in a variety of positions.
Appearances: 28+8 **Goals:** 7

Louis Dodds (top) scored seven goals while Tom Pope (bottom) managed to find the target 33 times [Photos: onevalefan.co.uk]

BEN WILLIAMSON: The pacy striker was another forward who linked up well with top-scorer Pope. Williamson earned himself a "supersub" title during the season thanks to his ability to come off the bench and grab a late goal.

Appearances: 11+27 **Goals:** 9

CALVIN ANDREW: The powerful striker was often used as a substitute by Micky Adams and thus he managed just the one goal – albeit the winner against Torquay United.

Appearances: 8+16 **Goals:** 1